Christmas

Christmas

Charles L. Allen

and

Charles L. Wallis

CHRISTMAS IN OUR HEARTS

CANDLE, STAR, AND CHRISTMAS TREE

WHEN CHRISTMAS CAME TO BETHLEHEM

FLEMING H. REVELL COMPANY
OLD TAPPAN, NEW JERSEY

Scripture quotations not otherwise identified in *Christmas in Our Hearts* are from the Revised Standard Version of the Bible, copyrighted 1946, 1952, © 1971 and 1973. Elsewhere they are from the King James Version of the Bible.

Acknowledgment is made to the following, who have granted permission for the reprinting of copyrighted material:

Abingdon Press for story from *The Village Tragedy* by Clovis G. Chappell; *The Atlantic Monthly* for "The Gift" by Laura Spencer Porter; The Christian Education Press for "Our Lady" by Edgar D. Kramer from *Tribute to Jesus;* Dodd, Mead & Company for "Lord of the Far Horizons" by Bliss Carman from *Bliss Carman's Poems,* and for "The Vigil of Joseph" by Elsa Barker; Harper & Brothers for "Childhood" by John Erskine, "Christmas at Babbitt's" by Henry H. Tweedy from *Masterpieces of Religious Verse,* copyright, 1948, by Harper & Brothers, and the extract from *One Fine Hour* by Frederick Keller Stamm, © 1954 by Harper & Brothers; the quotation from "Two Inscriptions for the Christmas Candle" by Anna Hempstead Branch, and the quotation from "Incarnation" by Edith Lovejoy Pierce from *Masterpieces of Religious Verse,* © 1948 by Harper & Brothers; Nancy Byrd Turner for her poem, "The Christmas Star"; World Call for "The Silent Stars Go By" by Harriet Hartridge Tompkins; *Good Housekeeping* for "Let Us Keep Christmas" by Grace Noll Crowell; Houghton Mifflin Company for "The Song of a Heathen" by Richard W. Gilder; Virgil Markham for "How the Great Guest Came" by Edwin Markham; Charles Scribner's Sons for "The Spirit of Christmas" by Henry van Dyke, material from *The Spirit of St. Louis* by Charles A. Lindbergh, "O World" by George Santayana.

Acknowledgment is gratefully made also for permission to reprint lines from "Journey of the Magi" from *Collected Poems of T. S. Eliot,* copyright, 1936, by Harcourt, Brace & World, Inc., and reprinted with their permission; from "The Death of the Hired Man" from *Complete Poems of Robert Frost,* copyright 1930, 1939, by Holt, Rinehart and Winston, Inc., and reprinted by permission of Holt, Rinehart and Winston, Inc.; from J.B. by Archibald MacLeish, 1958 and reprinted by permission of Houghton Mifflin Company; from "Credo" from *Collected Poems of Edwin Arlington Robinson,* copyright 1929, The Macmillan Company and used by permission; from "The Wisest of the Wise" from *Christmas Chimes in Rhyme* by Ralph W. Seager, © 1962 by The Judson Press and reprinted by permission of the author.

Library of Congress Cataloging in Publication Data

Allen, Charles Livingstone, date
   Christmas.

   CONTENTS: Christmas in our hearts.—Candle, star, and Christmas tree.—When Christmas came to Bethlehem.
   1. Christmas. 2. Jesus Christ—Nativity—Devotional literature. 3. Christmas—Meditations.
   I. Wallis, Charles Langworthy, 1921-   joint author.
   II. Title.
BV45.A53   232.9'21   77-22979
ISBN 0-8007-0874-1

Contents

When Christmas Came to Bethlehem

Preface

The many meanings of Christmas! Surely they are as numerous as the devout men, women, and children who gather year after year around the cradle in Bethlehem.

The outer splendor and sparkle of Christmas—seen and felt by everyone—increases as each generation makes its contribution. And how beautiful and ingenious these concentric circles of celebration have evolved! Generations yet to come will lovingly and imaginatively add *their* songs and stories, *their* rites and recipes.

But that which is seen by our eyes is little more than an outer and visible testimony of our hearts. Apart from our hearts' response to the love and divine grace given to us by God through His only begotten Son, the Lord Jesus, the ways in which we celebrate Christmas are, as Shakespeare said, "Full of sound and fury, signifying nothing."

Sometimes we are challenged to get Christ back into Christmas. But Christ never left Christmas, for Christmas is not expendable in God's plan and purpose of redemption. The real challenge is to get the Christ of Christmas into our hearts at Christmas—and ever after—so that He may reign where He most desires to reign—within our lives.

The pages which follow—written over a span of years and now brought together in a single volume— represent a journey of the spirit, a reopening of the wells our fathers dug, and a rekindling of the hearth fires that have given warmth and beauty throughout the years. Here are once more related the ultimate meanings of Christmas as proclaimed in Gospel text, hallowed by sacred tradition and custom, and communicated enthusiastically, inspirationally, and prayerfully by people convinced that "the hopes and fears of all the years are met in thee tonight."

CHARLES L. ALLEN
CHARLES L. WALLIS

Christmas

Christmas
in Our Hearts

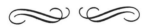

1

Christmas Is a Simple Story

The Christmas story is serenely simple. It cannot be complicated with philosophizing or with argument; it defies analysis and silences calculation. It is as simple as the silent dawn, as unbelabored as the bursting rose, as unsophisticated as a child's cry, as spontaneous as a child's laughter.

God through the centuries has manifested Himself in diverse and complex ways. We see an evidence of Him in the perfection of a mathematical formula and in the order of a distant galaxy; we hear Him speak through the profound utterances of noble minds and in the erudite thoughts of great theologians. But Christmas is like none of these. Christmas is as simple as childhood and as beautiful.

When God made His most benevolent gesture of fatherly love, His giving of a Son, He wanted to be understood by all men. But no flaming chariot bore Jesus from highest heaven. No mighty cannonade announced His appearing. There were no bugles, no treading of armies, none of the grandeur and glory we should devise for so remarkable an event.

Rather, silently and unobtrusively, Christ entered our world in the way each of us has come, as a weak

and helpless child. Why? When surely legions of
angels might have heralded His approach, why did
God choose from the most obscure of villages the most
unpretentious of maidens? Was it not that by sharing
our nature, His Son would speak our language, understand our homes, sympathize with our heartaches,
comprehend our hopes? Had He come in grandeur,
He would have been for us an unapproachable object
of wonder and awe. Had He come as a mighty con-
queror, we should have honored Him, but we would
also have feared Him.

> To be Himself a star most bright
> To bring the wise men to His sight,
> To be Himself a voice most sweet
> To call the shepherds to His feet,
> To be a child—it was His will,
> That folk like us might find Him still.
>
> JOHN ERSKINE

And yet is there in all creation a more miraculous
evidence of God's creatorship than a newborn baby?
Is there in all the vast reaches of the universe a more
wonderful expression of divine love than the child's
first cry?

The divine messenger who announced to Mary the
word of His coming said, ". . . the power of the Most
High will overshadow you; therefore the child to be
born will be called holy, the Son of God" (Luke 1:35).
A holiness attends all births, and the promise which
every newborn child brings to a mother's heart is an
evidence of God's love.

Christ came into the world as a baby. He left the world thirty-three brief years later when He was in the vigor and beauty of noble and consecrated young manhood. From that day to this, there has been no more wonderful expression of God's heart than the promise of childhood and the fulfillment of maturity. All life has become more precious, more consecrated and less expendable because of Him who has shown us the possibilities that lie within our human nature.

Christmas is a simple story, divinely simple yet profoundly inspiring, showing what life may mean for each of us.

2

The High Road of the Spirit

Many roads lead to Bethlehem. Mary and Joseph journeyed from Nazareth along roads crowded by people from many villages, who, at the command of Caesar, were to be enrolled. The wise men crossed the desert wastelands. The shepherds sought new wonders along the familiar hometown byways. But the first road to Bethlehem is unlike all other roads. It is the highway of preparation, spanning time and circumstance. It is the high road of the spirit.

Christmas did not just happen. For centuries men had anticipated Christmas in their hearts, looking forward eagerly to that hour of destiny when in the fullness of time God would reveal Himself in a more wondrous way than ever before.

The road of faith is an ancient road—and at times a dangerous and a narrow one. It was not always crowded nor were there always travelers upon it, yet along it moved men of adventurous spirit and women of the pilgrim heart. These knew it was God's highway and, although they could not discern their destination, they knew that their traveling was in the companionship of the Eternal. So they walked hopefully, expectantly, perhaps recalling the assurance of the psalmist, "Thou dost show me the path of life . . ." (Psalms 16:11).

The need of common men for God led them on. The prophet had promised, "I [God] will lead the blind in a way that they know not, in paths that they have not known I will guide them. I will turn the darkness before them into light, the rough places into level ground . . ." (Isaiah 42:16). Those who were spiritually blind hoped for a day of spiritual vision; those who were despondent or timid awaited a day of light. For surely ". . . the path of the righteous is like the light of dawn, which shines brighter and brighter until full day" (Proverbs 4:18).

Long before Christmas, God prepared His people. How the words of the prophets radiate a faith in the coming of the Wonderful Counsellor and the Prince of Peace! How the lives of men were changed, generation after generation, as men of faith journeyed toward the day of hope! The way of the Lord was built with human sighs and human aspirations and at the end of the road was a manger. From that manger lead all the roads of our lives.

The Divine Roadbuilder is God. If we follow the route He has mapped for our lives, we too will find a glory at our road's end. There may be detours, hazards and delays, but the highway of the Lord leads to the heights of vision and promise.

God guided many faithful persons to Bethlehem. He still leads all who will follow His guidance.

Lord of the far horizons,
Give us the eyes to see
Over the verge of sundown
The beauty that is to be.
Give us the skill to fashion
The task of Thy command,
Eager to follow the pattern
We may not understand.

BLISS CARMAN

3

Journey to Bethlehem

Nazareth, the home of Mary and Joseph, was nestled in a fold of the hills of lower Galilee from whose heights Joseph could look upon a panorama which extended a score or more miles in three directions. The lowlands teemed with activity; great caravan routes could be seen in the distance. People had left important centers of activity and they moved on toward the great commercial centers which Joseph knew only by hearsay.

Nazareth was not the kind of town about which people boast. "Can anything good come out of Nazareth?" (John 1:46) was no doubt a typical attitude of those who resided in more fortunate locations. But Nazareth was Joseph's home where he had long lived and where, perhaps, when he died he would be laid with his fathers nearby.

Nothing much happens in a town like Nazareth. Yet it was in that unlikely spot that a meek man and a humble young woman inherited the earth, for it was there that the Lord made Himself known to Joseph and to Mary. These common persons had an uncommon faith in God and in His purposes. They believed what the lords of the earth would have doubted. Through them a glory came to Nazareth, and because of them Nazareth has been spoken of with reverence through the centuries.

Because of his great faith, Joseph accepted Mary as only great faith and love can. Anxiously and lovingly he prepared for the birth of her Child. But his best-laid plans for her comfort and convenience were rudely interrupted, for "In those days a decree went out from Caesar Augustus that all the world should be enrolled" (Luke 2:1). Joseph could not expect the arm of Rome to be withdrawn merely because a Jewish maiden was soon to give birth to a child, so he left his home and woodworking shop and journeyed with Mary to Bethlehem that they might register their names on the census rolls.

The wise men traveled from the distant east, but presumably their trip was not without some measure of creature comfort, for they were men of wealth. Joseph was poor and little could he offer to Mary in the way of travel conveniences. No doubt he walked by the side of a small beast of burden upon which Mary rode. The road from Nazareth to Bethlehem was rough and hard, the dusty way probably crowded with many weary travelers, for all Galilee moved toward the city of David.

The road was tediously long, some eighty-five miles' distance. But they did not travel alone for on that road to Bethlehem they were companioned by God and guided by His Spirit. Always the steps of a good man are ordered by the Lord. Always the Lord of highest heaven dwells also with those who have humble and contrite hearts.

At last they came into the City of David, honored in history and rich in legend, but there was none to offer hospitality to them, and the only resting place they could secure was in a stable. The road to Bethlehem did not end in that shadowed stable, for from that humble spot, brightened for a moment by a splendor of Oriental wise men and restive shepherds, there came One who was to become the Guide for the spiritual pilgrimages of millions of the common children of the earth.

4

The Mother God Chose

Of all the women of history, the most honored and revered is Mary, the mother of Jesus. She stands apart from all other women; none is to be compared with her. Mary has been exalted in poetry, fiction and drama; her face is seen on canvas, in bronze, marble and stained glass and we prize the lovely hymns and carols that sing of her. She is enthroned within our own hearts.

> Our Lady is the music
> Of brooks and birds and bees,
> Of little children's laughter,
> Of blooming clover leas,
> Of larks and leaves and lilacs,
> Of grass and wind and rain;
> Our Lady is the music
> That solaces my pain.
>
> Our Lady is the beauty
> Of moon and star and sun,
> Of dawning on the roses,
> Of dusk when day is done,
> Of little children dancing

Where lilies lift and nod;
Our Lady is the beauty
That fills my soul with God.

EDGAR DANIEL KRAMER

True are the words of the angel, ". . . blessed art thou among women" (Luke 1:28).

Who was Mary? What kind of person was she? What life did she live? It is generally believed that she was directly descended from David. According to ancient tradition, her parents were Joachim and Anna, very devout and holy people. Mary was reared according to the faith of her fathers, and no doubt she was particularly sensitive to the voice and will of God. When the angel told her of God's plans for her life, Mary replied, "Behold I am the handmaid of the Lord; let it be to me according to your word . . ." (Luke 1:38). The literal meaning of the Greek word which we translate as "handmaid" is "a woman slave." Mary was in bondage to God's purposes; His will was her will.

When Mary first appears in the drama of the nativity, she is an obscure peasant girl of, perhaps, eighteen. No doubt her hands were rough and red from housework in a poor home. Today we see her pictured in the most costly garments; at her feet are laid the world's most precious jewels, yet never in her lifetime did she have more than the simplest necessities of life.

In appearance she may have been like many other Jewish maidens of her age. Nothing distinguished her from the others, yet the eternal God chose her from among humanity to be the mother of His Son. The birth of that Son is unmatched among the miracles of all time. We can no more explain His birth than we can explain the origins of the sun, the moon and the stars. When God sent an angel to tell Mary that she should bear a son she was puzzled and apprehensive. "How can this be," she asked, "since I have no husband?" (Luke 1:34). The angel told her of God's will.

At that time Mary was engaged to Joseph. When she discovered that she was with child, Joseph covered her shame with a blanket of love. St. Matthew says that Joseph, being a just man, was unwilling that she be made a public example. We admire Joseph's attitude for he might have been harsh and cruel. When the angel spoke to Joseph of Mary's innocence and said that her child was of God, Joseph understood and believed. When the Child was born, he named Him Jesus, as the angel had directed.

In later years, Jesus came to understand, too. "He said to them, 'You are from below, I am from above; you are of this world, I am not of this world' " (John 8:23).

Mary's life was hard and difficult. Although the angel had said that she, among all women, was highly favored, hers was not the kind of favor that we want from God. A few days before her baby's birth, she was required to take a long, painful journey to Bethlehem. There were nights of sleeping on the ground along the way, days of riding uphill and down on the back of a donkey. Suppose that donkey misstepped and fell! Finally, in Bethlehem, no room was available. Even when new life stirred within her, only a dirty stable and the company of domestic animals were offered to her. There, in the bleak midwinter, she gave birth to the Son of God.

A few hours later another hard journey was required; because of the fears and suspicions of Herod she must flee her homeland. Through the land of the Philistines to Gaza she traveled, and then out across the measureless, hot desert. How she must have longed to be with her own people! Could not God have spared her this added burden? But she did not question God's will. Gently, lovingly, she cared for her precious Baby.

Finally she returned with Joseph to their home— but what a poor home it was, for Joseph's income was obtained from a one-man carpenter shop in an out-of-the-way village. In the words of Jesus we catch glimpses of the only home He ever knew. He recalled how a candle would light the entire house, how clothes were patched and later patches were patched. Into that little, one-room home were later born at least six other children, four boys and two or more girls. Mary was never to know a life of quiet or days of rest.

Joseph is mentioned only once after the story of Jesus' birth, when he took his family to Jerusalem when Jesus was twelve. He may have died soon thereafter, leaving Mary a penniless widow and mother of seven children. Those were years of drudgery and she lived in relative obscurity.

But for the Son of God she made a home, and that is what He needed. History records that France had sixty-nine kings of which number only three were loved by their subjects. Those three were the only kings who had been raised by their mothers, the others being reared by private tutors, governesses, all disinterested persons.

Mary maintained such a home that her Child found mental stimulation, physical well-being and a spiritual atmosphere. "Jesus increased in wisdom and in stature, and in favor with God and man" (Luke 2:52). The patched clothes were kept clean; the simple food was well prepared. We can imagine that Mary read to her children and talked with them about the problems of life, that she prayed with them about the open hearth and went with them to God's house to worship. That was the kind of home God chose for His Son.

The golden thread woven throughout the fabric of Mary's character is her beautiful and sincere humility. Engraved on her heart were the words of the angel, but this did not make her proud or boastful. When the innkeeper said that his establishment was already overcrowded, she might have said: "I demand the best you have. I am the mother of God." Instead, "Mary kept all these things, pondering them in her heart" (Luke 2:19).

When Jesus was twelve, we read of a misunderstanding between mother and Child. After the experience in the Temple, Jesus said, "How is it that you sought me? Did you not know that I must be in my Father's house?" (Luke 2:49). Mary was bewildered by His words, but she knew the Boy was growing up and breaking away naturally from the disciplines of His family. Sometimes parental love is selfish; sometimes it is jealous. Mary may have felt at times that she was being shut out of His life, but never did she feel mistreated and never did her Son hurt her.

At the wedding in Cana, we see Mary with Jesus. Some biblical scholars surmise that this may have been the wedding of one of Jesus' sisters. After that hour, however, Mary remains discreetly in the background. On one occasion, while Jesus is speaking to the multitudes, ". . . his mother and his brothers came; and standing outside they sent to him and called him" (Mark 3:31). Such was the manner of the mother God chose. She did not dominate; she did not demand. She gave of herself freely, but she was wise enough to know when to cut the apron strings.

Mary never doubted God. She remained loyal through the years. Then came a day when she heard a mob cry, "Crucify him!" She stayed close by. We read, ". . . standing by the cross of Jesus . . . [was] his mother . . ." (John 19:25). As the nails pierced His hands, they pierced her heart. Poor little mother, how hard the path God gave to her! How strangely the night in Bethlehem had been transformed. When Jesus, from the cross, saw His mother, He gently called to His dearest friend, "Behold your mother . . . ." And to Mary He said, "Woman, behold your son!" (John 19:26, 27). The disciple placed his arm about Mary and spoke comfortingly to her broken spirit.

The last glimpse we have of Mary is in the upper room where she prays with those who believe in Him. Her faith in God has been vindicated. Victory has dispelled the clouds.

There is no record of the time or the manner of her

death, and we do not know where she was finally laid to rest. Perhaps it is as well, for just as her Son continues to live in our midst, so too does her gentle life continue to inspire mothers everywhere.

As we remember the mother God chose, dare we not believe that He may be choosing us for His service? We do not ask that our way be easy or that we always understand all that happens. We only ask that we be strong to give our best and to remain ever true, even as Mary was.

5

Joseph, Son of David

Little is known about Joseph of Nazareth. He is spoken of briefly in the Gospels of Matthew, Luke and John, but he is mentioned nowhere else in the Scriptures. Matthew calls him a just man.

In a deep sleep he heard the voice of a messenger from the Lord who said to him: "Joseph, son of David, do not fear to take Mary as your wife, for that which is conceived in her is of the Holy Spirit; she will bear a son, and you shall call his name Jesus, for he will save his people from their sins." And Joseph ". . . did as the angel of the Lord commanded him . . ." (Matthew 1:20, 21, 24).

Joseph was descended from King David and his family home was Bethlehem. What mighty wonders of old are mirrored in him—but none so wondrous as God's purpose for him at this later hour. He apparrently had migrated to Nazareth where he established himself in the trade of carpentry and where in time he was engaged to Mary, a maiden of that community. He was at Mary's side when Jesus was born. Perhaps these words best express Joseph's mind that holy night:

After the Wise Men went, and the strange star
Had faded out, Joseph the father sat
Watching the sleeping Mother and the Babe,
And thinking stern, sweet thoughts the long night
     through.

"Ah, what am I, that God has chosen me
To bear this blessed burden, to endure
Daily the presence of this loveliness,
To guide this Glory that shall guide the world?

"Brawny these arms to win Him bread, and broad
This bosom to sustain her. But my heart
Quivers in lonely pain before the Beauty
It loves—and serves—and cannot understand!"

ELSA BARKER

When the wrath of Herod was kindled against Jesus, Joseph took Mary and the Child and together they sought safety in Egypt. Later the three returned to Nazareth, and the hand of Joseph protected and provided for the growing Boy. When Jesus was twelve years old, the devout father journeyed with Mary and Jesus to the Temple in Jerusalem.

Nothing more is given in the Bible by which we may complete the tapestry of Joseph's life, although tradition says that he was considerably older than Mary and that he died during Jesus' childhood. Soon, however, Jesus assumed the responsibility of the household and probably also followed the carpenter's trade. His family obligations may account for the fact that Jesus delayed His public ministry until the age of thirty.

A few biblical references and a scattered account from tradition are all we can know of Joseph. But are there not some details which our imaginations may add?

Joseph was, first of all, a God-fearing man who was loyal to the God of his fathers and faithful to their religious practices. Jesus, in His formative years, learned from Joseph the great lessons of faith and morality, of love toward man and God, of service and sacrifice.

Everything we know of Joseph suggests that he was a loving and devoted husband. The teachings of Jesus concerning love for family and neighbor reflect His home training and discipline. The highest compliment which we can pay to Joseph is found in Jesus' teaching that men should call God their heavenly Father. Would this image have come from the lips of Jesus if He had not already known the love and care, the protection and concern of an earthly father?

A little boy, who had been cast in the role of Joseph in a Christmas play, complained that he did not have a "speaking part." Joseph had a silent, though very important role in the drama of salvation. Do not "They also serve who only stand and wait"? On the first Christmas Joseph, silent and stalwart, stood at the side of Mary. When God called upon him, he did as the Lord had bidden him.

6

There Were Shepherds

The shepherds of Bethlehem did not have far to travel. The wise men followed the dusty caravan routes that led from their eastern countries, but the shepherds did not need to travel by day and night along strange and sometimes dangerous roads. Christmas came to them. Christ was born in their home town and to see Him, the shepherds walked along familiar streets.

High above the roads of Bethlehem the shepherds were tending their sheep, a task often dull and monotonous. One night must have seemed the same as a thousand others. Occasionally there would be a stir among the sheep, and the shepherds would move among the flocks to see if there was trouble, returning to the open fire where they would try to keep warm as they again listened to the yarns and tales which herdsmen had told each other for generations. These common shepherds were doing their duty, as they understood it, by protecting their sheep and earning a meager subsistence for their families.

Then into the midst of their routine lives came a glowing, amazing experience. God pierced the shadows of their common task with a light not of this world and with a message for the ages. Angels sang of wonderful good news and the shepherds went in haste to Bethlehem.

Our lives are like that, too. In our daily living unexpected wonders constantly appear. Here we are, doing our duty with what faithfulness we can muster, and then suddenly life glows. The unexpected happens, our lives take on new dimensions. Never again do our days seem quite so plain.

The shepherds did not question that God had actually manifested Himself to them, for they immediately left the mountainside and hurried into the streets they had walked since childhood. An ordinary day had become extraordinary, and now a town they had known so long became more than commonplace, too. Probably in their hearts those shepherds many times had envied those who journeyed from strange, exotic places and had longed for the day when they too might travel to the golden lands beyond the horizon.

But on Christmas Eve no such wanderlust lingered in their minds. God had come to them. Their home town seemed wonderfully alive with a glory they had never seen before.

Two things stand out in the story of the shepherds. First, any day may become a special day if we have the heart to see its wonders. Second, any town will become more than marvelous to the man who seeks for evidences of God's presence along the most familiar byways.

7

They Saw His Star

At the top of our Christmas trees most of us fix a star, for in the heavens, high over Bethlehem, there was a star.

The star is an especially meaningful symbol for Christmas. Stars speak of other worlds; their radiance comes from afar and they testify to a realm beyond our earth. Christmas has just such a message for each of us. Above our busy lives, high over our varied activities and above our doubts and fears, there is a Spirit that presides and counsels, plans and guides.

Long before science gave to men exact ways of measuring celestial distances, for reckoning time, for finding directions on endless deserts and on vast oceans, men looked to the stars, and a sense of certainty came into their lives. The stars are constant and dependable; an astronomer can predict with surety their movements, ascertaining what position a particular star maintained a thousand years ago, and foretelling its movements during a thousand years to come. It is good to know that something is certain, something is steadfast. Human beings are fickle. Our steps turn at the slightest whim; our plans are altered by the weakest argument. But God, like the stars He created, is eternal and steadfast, the same yesterday, today and forever. Like the stars in His heavens, God challenges our weakness by His dependability.

The stars are most clearly seen when it is night. When the earth is darkest, they shine with greatest brilliance. Just so, when we are overwhelmed by clouds of despondency and when our lives are shrouded in a night of fear, then we see most clearly the light of God's truth and the brightness of His all-comprehending love. Could the Almighty have chosen a more suitable or appropriate symbol for Christmas than a star?

The Wise Men were guided by a star. From their homes they traveled in its light. They did not know the way and they were not sure of their destination but they believed the star, for to them the star represented God's guiding hand. On the night of Christ's birth the Bethlehem star was high above the heads of every man. All men could have seen it, but the wise men followed it. In their hearts was a compelling faith that is a prerequisite for all star-led journeys. If we believe in God, He will guide our steps aright. When we trust Him, He will make bright the way ahead. He who stands among us still is ". . . the bright morning star" (Revelation 22:16).

8

There Came Wise Men From the East

The celebration of Christmas is always given a certain regal glamour by the story of the Wise Men, who, journeying long days and weary nights across waste land and desert, came at last to Bethlehem to pledge fealty to the newborn King Jesus. Theirs was the most complicated itinerary of all those who traveled to Bethlehem. Yet, long as their journey may have been, only a few pen strokes in a single chapter in Matthew chronicle their experiences. But how colorful is this story, and how much the Wise Men add to the drama of Christ's nativity!

They are called Wise Men because by profession and study they had mastered both the lore of books and the wisdom of the heavens; they were philosophers and astrologers. In that day astrologers observed the heavens in order to determine the will of God. The Wise Men had long accustomed themselves to look above the world of men for guidance from the Most High and their behavior was formed not by the foibles and folly of men but by the wisdom of God.

I imagine that those "kings of the east" were objects of ridicule and scorn when they first announced to their friends that they planned to make a long journey to a strange land to worship a new king. Many centuries before Noah had been laughed at when, in obedience to God, he fashioned an ark and prepared for a flood.

There are other thoughts which our imaginations kindle, for biographical information about the Wise Men is not available to us. No names are recorded nor do we know from what countries they journeyed. Legend has, however, given us some grand and wonderful details. Legend says that they were kings of eastern monarchies. This is a reasonable presumption, for they brought royal gifts to the Child; they paused long enough at Herod's palace to pay their respects to the local ruler after the fashion of visiting potentates; and, finally, they came asking for One who would be King of the Jews, before whom they knelt. There is no particular reason for limiting their number to three; this number was probably based on the fact that three gifts were presented to Christ. An early tradition says that the kings traveled with a vast retinue of which seven thousand men were left beyond the Euphrates and more than a thousand continued on to Jerusalem. An ancient tradition also assigns names to the kings.

Caspar, Melchior, Balthazar,
These are they who followed the star.

Myrrh, and incense, gems and gold,
These are the gifts they brought of old.

These are the precious, wonderful things
They brought, as befitting three wise kings.
LAURA SPENCER PORTER

The gifts are not without a spiritual significance. Melchior offered gold in recognition of the Child's royalty. Gaspar, or Caspar, presented frankincense, symbolic of Christ's divinity. Balthazar laid before the manger a gift of myrrh, emblematic of the Passion of our Lord. Such is the rich embroidery of legend and lore.

The Wise Men were wise not only because of their learning but because they were obedient to the heavenly vision. When God showed them a star, they followed its gleam. George Santayana was thinking of this kind of wisdom when he wrote:

> O world, thou choosest not the better part!
> It is not wisdom to be only wise,
> And on the inward vision close the eyes;
> But it is wisdom to believe the heart.
> Columbus found a world, and had no chart
> Save one that faith deciphered in the skies;
> To trust the soul's invincible surmise
> Was all his science and his only art.
> Our knowledge is a torch of smoky pine
> That lights the pathway but one step ahead
> Across a void of mystery and dread.
> Bid, then, the tender light of faith to shine
> By which alone the mortal heart is led
> Unto the thinking of the thought divine.
>
> GEORGE SANTAYANA

The Wise Men of old believed because their hearts were attuned to God. Men are wise today when, kneeling at the crib of the Child Jesus, they surrender their human wisdom to the influence of the greater wisdom of God.

Not only were the Magi men of wisdom; they were also men of courage who left their faraway homes to journey into an unknown adventure. When they had prepared themselves for travel, they challenged heroically the winds and the dangers of the desert. Such courage has ever been one of the essential ingredients of Christian discipleship.

To the wisdom and courage of these men must be added faith. First, they trusted God and His guidance. Second, when they found the new King, they knelt to worship and adore. Third, they again depended on God to lead them back to their homes "by another way." From Bethlehem they trekked beyond history. Yet for one hushed moment they entered into the gospel story before passing from history—to remain in the hearts and imaginations of mankind. Their faith remains to stir and to challenge us.

In the birth of Christ is fulfilled all of the wisdom of the ages. The Wise Men knew that the heavens declared the glory of God. We too are wise when, like them, we look upward and when, having discerned the heavenly sign, we follow where it leads. God often makes known His will to men, but only those who are wise respond to His guidance.

9

His Name Emmanuel

The most persistent quest of mankind has been for a more perfect knowledge of God. "Oh, that I knew where I might find him!" (Job 23:3) is the longing not only of Job but also of the deepest recesses of the human spirit. Again and again this desire is found in the Psalms. "My soul longs . . . my heart and flesh sing for joy to the living God" (Psalms 84:2). "My soul thirsts for God, for the living God. When shall I come and behold the face of God?" (Psalms 42:2).

When we have passed into some valley of the shadow, when we cling desperately to straws, when all doors close and the night of grief, or sorrow, or despair seems eternally dark—then we hunger and thirst for God. Or when at some moment of achievement we discern more clearly the road ahead or find at last the heights which rise above normal daily living—then too we desire the companionship of the Lord. I doubt if there was ever a man who did not, at one time or another, look anxiously into the heavens or longingly into the depths of his heart for some reflection of God. It is proverbial that even the skeptic or agnostic at the moment of death asks for spiritual consolation.

God has in innumerable ways revealed Himself to those who have opened their eyes to see His ministrations, or opened their ears to hear His voice, or opened their hearts to His Spirit. God has revealed Himself through inspired spokesmen, through great books and the Book, through a casual word providently offered by a friend, through an insight which breaks suddenly and with enlightenment within our minds. God is revealed supremely for Christians in and through Jesus Christ.

The message of the Advent season is found in the words, ". . . his name shall be called Emmanuel (which means, God with us)" (Matthew 1:23). Jesus said, ". . . He who has seen me has seen the Father . . ." (John 14:9). What we know of the character and nature of God we know through His Son; in Him God is with us. St. Paul affirms this: "For God who said, 'Light shall shine out of darkness,' has shone within my heart to illuminate men with the knowledge of God's glory in the face of Christ" (2 Corinthians 3:6, MOFFATT).

Christmas brings many joys, but none is greater than the knowledge that we have in the Babe of Bethlehem a reflection of God. Joseph Fort Newton once wrote of Christmas, "For the first time man was glad about God." What he meant is that through Christ so many anxious questions have been answered and so many longings have been fulfilled that fear and doubt have given way to exaltation and gladness. For each of us the gospel of Christ is the good news about God.

10

God's Inexpressible Gift

This verse seems particularly appropriate at Christmas: "Thanks be to God for his inexpressible gift" (2 Corinthians 9:15). Our Christmas tradition of gift-giving stems from the benevolence of God who has given many gifts to His children. We might speak of the world in which we live as a gift from Him. And there are the gifts of loving friends, smiling children, the beauties of the changing seasons, the promise of day and the rest of night, hope in a world filled with despair, the offer of salvation. Most precious is God's gift of Christ and His life, His teaching, His abiding presence in the heart.

Through our exchange of gifts we emulate in a small way the Spirit of God. When our giving is determined by love and sincerity we share the Spirit of God and, I believe, God blesses our gifts.

But Christmas is more than the giving of gifts. It is the adjusting of all of life to the will of God. A great preacher of an earlier generation, Henry van Dyke, points to the truth of this through a series of questions:

Are you willing to forget what you have done for other people, and to remember what other people have done for you; to ignore what the

world owes you, and to think what you owe the world; to put your rights in the background, and your duties in the foreground; to own that probably the only good reason for your existence is not what you are going to get out of life, but what you are going to give to life; to close your book of complaints against the management of the universe, and look around you for a place where you can sow a few seeds of happiness—are you willing to do these things even for a day? Then you can keep Christmas.

A window atop Mount Tom in Massachusetts contains four panes of glass, each of a different color. Through the pane of brown glass one sees a picture of the Berkshire Hills which resembles the beauties of autumn. Winter is suggested by what one sees through the blue glass. The pane of green glass gives to the hills beyond the youthfulness of spring. And a summer sunset is seen when one looks through the pane of red glass. Always, however, the same Berkshire Hills are in view.

So it is with Christmas. One man, greedy for financial gain, thinks of Christmas as a time for exploitation. A sensuous man considers Christmas as a day for indulgence. Another makes Christmas an occasion for getting presents. But the Christian is reminded that beyond and above all else Christmas is God's inexpressible gift of love, and brotherhood, and good will, and Christ. Reminded of this, his life is attuned to God and made beautiful as he welcomes into his heart the love of God in Christ Jesus.

11

The Wonder of It All

The Christmas experience is so overwhelming that our minds cannot comprehend all of it. No one person sees every facet. On the first Christmas the wise men saw a star which the shepherds missed, but the shepherds heard the singing of angels which the wise men did not hear. Mary pondered in her heart thoughts too deep for the shepherds, and Simeon discerned in Christ a religious significance that even Mary did not perceive. No one sees all of Christmas, but if I were to choose any one perspective it would be that of the shepherds.

They were simple men. When, on the hillside, they were frightened by a great heavenly light, an angel calmed their fears and told of a Baby who had been born. They hurried to Bethlehem and worshiped Christ, becoming the first persons on earth to celebrate Christmas. Then we read, "The shepherds returned, glorifying and praising God for all they had heard and seen . . ." (Luke 2:20).

In one way or another nearly all of us celebrate Christmas. What will you get from Christmas? Some will get only a hangover and a headache. Others will get a load of debts. Some will get only a day free from work and an opportunity to sleep late. But many will experience the thrill of giving loving gifts to dear ones and of reading the notes on greeting cards.

Best of all are the blessings which Christmas brought to the shepherds. Their first blessing was a sense of wonder. Charles A. Lindbergh, during his famous flight across the Atlantic, recorded:

> It's hard to be an agnostic up here in the Spirit of St. Louis, aware of the frailty of man's devices, a part of the universe between its earth and stars. If one dies, all this goes on existing in a plan so perfectly balanced, so wonderfully simple, so incredibly complex that it's far beyond our comprehension—worlds and moons revolving; planets orbiting on suns; suns flung with recklessness through space. There's the infinite magnitude of the universe; there's the infinite detail of its matter—the outer star, the inner atom. And man conscious of it all a worldly audience to what—if not to God.

Christmas gathers up the happy celebrations of many different people: the joy of the sun worshipers in the return of the light and warmth of the sun-god; the fir tree of pre-Christian German festivities; the Yule log from Iceland; the mistletoe from pre-Christian England; Santa Claus, saint of Holland. To these is added the wonder which the shepherds experienced. Oh, the wonder of Him who means so much to so many people and adds depth of joy to so many traditions! The eternal God come to earth—that is wonderful.

Welcome! all Wonders in one sight!
  Eternity shut in a span.
Summer in winter, day in night,
  Heaven in earth, and God in man.
Great little one! whose all-embracing birth
  Lifts earth to heaven, stoops heav'n to earth!
                                    RICHARD CRASHAW

The shepherds' second blessing was an inner warmth. They returned to their fields with a song in their hearts. Isn't it remarkable how Christmas still warms even the coldest hearts? Despite Caesar's decree, the weary journey of a peasant couple, the order of Herod that the children be slaughtered—the impression of the first Christmas is one of joy and love. Even today the hearts of men beat more in unison at Christmas than at any other time.

We have become accustomed to the reports of those operations wherein surgeons ask healthy persons to "lend" their hearts to patients. The surgeons operate on the idle heart of one man while life is maintained through the heartbeat of the other, as the blood flows through the plastic tubes that connect their bodies. What a perfect picture of what the spirit of Christmas does. We lend our hearts to others through understanding, and sympathy, and goodwill. At Christmas a cold heart is out of place.

Third, the shepherds found someone to worship. They bowed not to a god whom they feared or from whom they should flee, but they knelt at the crib of a God of love. Man's heart seeks a God like that.

E. Stanley Jones tells of a little boy, the son of missionary parents, who was in school in the United States at Christmas. His parents were far away. When a teacher asked the boy what he most wanted for Christmas, the lad looked at a framed picture of his father on his desk and then replied, "I want my father to step out of that frame!" The eternal God stepped from His celestial frame and came close to man at Bethlehem. Now men could know, and reach, and love God.

At Christmas we may find the shepherds' blessings. We too may be caught up in the wonder of it all and find that inner warmth which sets our hearts aglow. We may lift our hearts in adoration and sing, "Glory to God in the highest."

12

Flight by Night

There is an epilogue to the high drama of the Christmas story. It brings the story of the angel's song, the wise men's visit and the joy of Mary's heart back to the rough realities of the world in which we live. The epilogue is tragic, and perhaps only those who have been ruthlessly uprooted by fear and prejudice in our day can fully appreciate the flight of Joseph, Mary and the Child into Egypt. St. Matthew relates tersely the blunt facts: "Now when they [the Wise Men] had departed, behold, an angel of the Lord appeared to Joseph in a dream and said, 'Rise, take the child and his mother, and flee to Egypt, and remain there till I tell you; for Herod is about to search for the child, to destroy him.' And he rose and took the child and his mother by night, and departed to Egypt, and remained there until the death of Herod . . ." (Matthew 2:13–15).

Herod, whose life and actions anticipated the cruel despotism of our generation, had sought to obtain from the Wise Men information about Him who was born to be King of the Jews. The Wise Men, led by God, returned to their homes without informing Herod. Herod's wrath waxed hot. He ordered the slaying of all children, lest the One among them might some day challenge his authority. But God once more revealed His will to Joseph, and the holy family departed, under the cloak of darkness, for refuge in a foreign land.

It is strange how life so often dashes us from the heights of joy to the lowlands of despair, from the mountaintops of vision to the valleys of sorrow. This was the bewildering experience of the holy family. One night a star stood high above them, but the next night every shadow was potentially dangerous; from behind a rock or a tree might step one of Herod's informers.

But the Lord God, whom Joseph had obeyed all of his life and whom Mary had loved with a constant faithfulness, did not abandon them in their hour of danger. Very often, in the years that followed, Mary told her Child of the ways in which God always attends His children in their great need. That Child's faith in God never was to waver in an hour of trouble when His friends left nor in an hour of trial when He stood alone with God. We naturally trust God when life moves smoothly, when the waters of experience are untroubled, when the wind brushes gently against our cheeks. But trust in God is even more needful when dangers threaten and when calamity falls with a heavy thud upon our lives. Mary and Joseph knew that God was with them in the stable, and they knew too that they were within His encircling love when they followed the rough road of escape to Egypt.

The Herod of the Christmas chronicle is Herod the Great, who fought his way to power with a strong arm and a clever head. He was zealous and fanatic; fear and suspicion were his masters. He was a despot who cajoled his subjects and ultimately persecuted members of his own family. His was the order which put to death his wife Mariamne and two of their sons. History has given him the benevolent title of "Herod the Great" because he was an empire builder, but he passed to his children a legacy of craftiness and passion. His second son, Herod Antipas, was tetrarch when Jesus was crucified.

"But when Herod died . . ." (Matthew 2:19). The words have the dull, cold, impersonal character of rock. How final are the words which mark Herod's passing in the pages of Scripture. It is like a great sigh of relief. It marks the end of a tyrannical rule. The folly of man had spent itself.

Joseph then took his family into Galilee and once again he returned to his Nazareth home. There ". . . the child grew and became strong, filled with wisdom; and the favor of God was upon him" (Luke 2:40).

13

As We Leave Bethlehem

Christmas has come and gone. Soon the decorations will be carefully packed away until another year. The elusive pine needles will be swept up. The children will be sent back to school. The thank-you notes will be written and the warm and glowing experience will become a memory.

Some people are also likely to put into a deep freezer their cheerfulness and good will. The boss will become as cranky as ever. People will become themselves once more. But it was good to see what a change could be wrought in the minds and hearts of men, even for a day! Yet Christmas need not be limited to only a day. Christmas can become, as it was meant to be, an attitude toward life that will continue during all of the days that follow.

The roads to Bethlehem were roads of hope and trust, of faith and charitableness. Bethlehem is not a dead end; it is rather the place from which we move with greater goodwill, deeper faith, more permanent peace of mind and heart. Joseph Fort Newton wrote:

Christmas is a prophetic day, looking not so much backward as forward. It belongs to an order of life not yet attained, to a religion not yet realized; to a coming, but distant, time which all prophets have foreseen, when men will be ruled by "the angels of our higher nature," and justice will reign, and pity and joy will walk the common ways of life.

The Bible tells us not only of those who went to Bethlehem, but also of those who went away. The shepherds were watching their sheep on the hills roundabout Bethlehem when in a vision splendid they were told of Christ's birth. They hastened to His manger. Then they returned to their flocks, ". . . glorifying and praising God for all they had heard and seen . . ." (Luke 2:20). Their rejoicing could not be extinguished with the coming of sunrise on the day after Christmas. Their joy was eternal. Around their camp fires they rehearsed again and again the experiences until, I am sure, their lives, their homes, their work radiated with a continuing joyfulness.

The wise men had stopped at Herod's palace on their journey to Bethlehem. He asked them to visit him before they returned, but ". . . being warned in a dream not to return to Herod, they departed to their own country by another way" (Matthew 2:12). And they returned by a different spiritual way; the old way of life was no longer satisfying. They had found in Bethlehem a new and a better way to live.

As we leave Bethlehem, we ought to leave behind old grudges, old fears, old sorrows. We ought to continue our adventure of life praising God and by walking on new and better roads. Sometime during the winter we shall need the friendly spirit of Christmas. Sometime in the spring we shall want the hope of Christmas. Let us not pack up the true spirit of Christmas when we put away the decorations.

14

Some Never Know He Came

"When the angels went away from them into heaven, the shepherds said to one another . . ." (Luke 2:15). What did they say? What do we say on the day after Christmas? For weeks we anticipate Christmas. We buy gifts and cards, we attend parties and we decorate our homes. We sing carols and contribute to special charities and within our hearts is the spirit of goodwill and cheer. It is a happy time, but soon it is all over—or is it?

Suppose the shepherds had said: "Well, that was a thrilling experience. The choir from heaven and the words of the angel stirred our hearts. But let's get down to earth now. There are the sheep to be watched."

Or, as we might say: "Let's wash the dishes, clean up the house and get back on the job. There are bills to be paid and the things that have been neglected during the past days." What a shocking letdown!

Dr. Clovis G. Chappell has drawn an imaginary word-picture of one of those shepherds, who had been a youth on that first Christmas night and who now has become old. His grandson sits on his knee as he recalls: "A long, long time ago, when I was little more than a boy, I was out on the Judean hills one night with some other shepherds, keeping watch over the flock. And the angel of the Lord came upon us and the glory of the Lord shone roundabout us. And we were sore afraid. But the angel said, 'Fear not . . . for unto you is born this day in the city of David a Saviour, which is Christ the Lord . . . . You shall find the babe in swaddling clothes, lying in a manger.' "

The old man's lips cease to move, and there is silence. Then the lad turns and looks with wide, puzzled eyes into his grandfather's face and says: "But, granddaddy, is that all? What did you do when you heard the good news? Was what the angel said really true? Was the Christ Child ever really born?"

The old shepherd sadly shakes his white head and answers: "I never knew. I never went to see. Some say that it is all a myth. Others say they found in Him the light of God, the power for life. But for me, I could never be quite sure. I never did go to see."

The supreme tragedy of Christmas is that its real meaning is unknown or completely neglected by so many people. Millions who celebrate and live by a calendar that reckons time by His birth do not know Him.

On Christmas eve they filled the house, some fifty guests all
    told,
    (O little Lord of Christmas, were you left out in the cold?)

And ate and sang, played cards and danced till early morning light.
    (O little Lord of Christmas, did they think of you that
    night?)

Next morning came the presents on a glittering Christmas
      tree.
   (O little Lord of Christmas, was there any gift for thee?)

The dinner was a Roman feast, and how those guests did
      eat!
   (O little Lord of Christmas, were you hungry in the
   street?)

Then came some teas, a movie, and at night the last revue.
   (O little Lord of Christmas, what had these to do with
   you?)

By midnight all were tired and cross and tumbled into bed.
   (O little Lord of Christmas, did they think that you were
   dead?)

They all woke up with headaches and no joy in work or
      play.
   (O little Lord of Christmas, did they mark your birth that
   day?)

The love, the joy were good, no doubt; the rest a pagan
      spree.
   (O little Lord of Christmas, let us keep the day with thee!)
                              HENRY HALLAM TWEEDY

But there are others who through the study of His
Word and worship in the church He established have
consecrated their lives to His will. Like the
shepherds, they have said, ". . . Let us go over to
Bethlehem . . ." (Luke 2:15).

15

How to Keep Your Christmas Joy

My father used to have the most wonderful garden each year, and we always had fresh vegetables in great abundance. Mother, looking ahead to the cold winter days when the garden would be covered by dead leaves, spent many hours canning the beans, tomatoes and other good things. Then in the months that followed she would go to the pantry and take the jars from the shelves. She made it possible for us to have vegetables all year round.

Could we do something like that with the wonderful Christmas spirit? Perhaps we could store up the good feeling we have at Christmas and let a little of it loose in our lives on each of the days that follow. Let us see how it may be possible.

Christmas begins with a Baby. Bishop Arthur J. Moore tells of a group of men who, laboring in the woods of northwest Canada, were away from the sight of good women for many months. When their wives joined them, the men organized a celebration and brought in a band. Among the women who came was one who had brought her baby. When the band started to play, the baby became frightened and started to cry. A rough old woodsman jumped up and shouted, "Stop the band so we can hear the baby cry."

We remember how Herod tried his hardest to kill the baby Jesus by killing nearly all the babies of Bethlehem; but little Jesus had been slipped away. Suppose that Herod had succeeded in his attempt to kill Jesus. No one can measure what a difference in the history of the world that would have made. What a dreary world this would be without the baby Jesus!

As long as babies are born, the world has hope. Consider the year 1809, for example. It was a bleak and dismal time. A ruthless dictator seemed certain to conquer the world and there was almost no hope left in anyone's heart. One morning in February of that year a traveler walked into a country store in the mountains of Kentucky. He asked, "Anything new happen around here lately?" "Nothing ever happens around here," someone replied. "There was a baby born up at the Lincoln cabin last night—that's all." That was one of the most important things that ever happened in this great country of ours.

In that year other babies were born: Charles Darwin and Gladstone, Tennyson and Edgar Allan Poe, Cyrus McCormick and Mendelssohn. You never know what may happen in the world because a baby has been born.

At Christmas our pulses beat more quickly because we know the coming of that Baby has done more to soften the hardness of the world's heart, to bring hope in the midst of the world's despair and to bring joy in the midst of sadness, than any event that has ever taken place since the beginning of time. As we consider Him, our own hearts are softened and our lives are transformed. I wish we might think about that

Baby every day of the year; in that way we shall keep our Christmas joy.

The Bible says, "In him was life." We use the word "life" to describe so many things that we become confused concerning what life really is. A policeman tells me that if I ride with him on a single night's patrol, I will learn something about life. I will see drunks, fights and many of the unpleasant things that happen in a large city. "Until you see what I see," he says, "you haven't really seen life." But is that life?

In the cold winter we longingly read the alluring advertisements about Caribbean cruises. We picture ourselves sunning lazily on the deck of a steamer, listening to the romantic melodies of an orchestra. All our cares and problems vanish. "This is life," the advertisements read. But is it?

Death comes to our homes and takes away a dear loved one. Bravely we encourage each other by saying: "We must face up to this. This is life." Is it? A group throws a wild party and shouts, "This is life!" Is it? We look at a famous painting and exclaim, "It has life!" Is that life?

You see, when we say "life" we mean many different things. So, when John said, "In him was life," just what was he talking about? If we might know, then we would surely know a Christmas joy that can be cherished all year round.

The best known and loved of all Christmas stories, excepting only those in the Bible, is *A Christmas Carol* by Charles Dickens. This story describes more accurately than any other the life that the spirit of Christmas brings. Old Scrooge was a selfish, heartless man. But at Christmastime the air was charged with good cheer. We see it in the friendliness of Bob Cratchit and in the gentleness of Tiny Tim. At last even old Scrooge surrenders to the Christmas spirit; at Christmas, Ebenezer Scrooge found life.

Dr. Hughes Wagner once spoke to a little girl whose parents had separated. "Doesn't your dad ever come to see you?" he asked. "No," she answered. Then her face brightened and she added, "Except at Christmas. Every Christmas he comes." On that one day the little girl had a loving father. I don't know what that father did on other days, but I believe he came nearer to finding real life on Christmas than at any other time.

Alexander Woollcott told a story that came out of the First World War. One Christmas the Americans in the field heard German soldiers singing a familiar carol. The Americans joined in. They met under a flag of truce and on that battlefield they had a Christmas service, treating each other as friends. This was the spirit of Christmas at work. Certainly that day those men more nearly lived than when they were fighting each other.

"In him was life." Wouldn't it be wonderful if we might really live all through the year!

Especially at Christmas I enjoy reading Edwin Markham's story-poem about the coming of Christ. Conrad, the godly old cobbler, one night dreamed that Christ would come to his shop on the following day. Early the next morning Conrad went to the woods to gather green boughs to decorate his shop for the Lord's coming. All morning he waited, but the only visitor was an old man who asked if he might sit down to rest. Conrad saw that his shoes were worn. Before sending the stranger on his way, Conrad put on his feet the best pair in the shop.

Throughout the afternoon he waited for the Lord's coming, but the only person he saw was an old woman who struggled under a heavy load. Out of compassion, he brought her in and gave her some of the food he had prepared for Christ. She went on her way refreshed. Just as the shades of night were falling, a lost child entered his shop. Conrad carried the child home, and then hurried back lest he miss the coming of Christ. But though he waited long and patiently, Christ did not come. Finally, in disappointment, the old cobbler cried:

> "Why is it, Lord, that your feet delay?
> Did You forget that this was the day?"
> Then soft in the silence a Voice he heard:
> "Lift up your heart, for I kept my word.
> Three times I came to your friendly door;
> Three times my shadow was on your floor.
> I was the beggar with bruisèd feet;
> I was the woman you gave to eat;
> I was the child on the homeless street!"
>
> EDWIN MARKHAM

How can we keep our Christmas joy all the year? Loving service to others is part of the answer.

But to all of this must be added something more. A pastor in the midwest tells of a woman who came to him for healing. She said: "I have had a bad limp, and medical men say there is nothing they can do for me. I wish you would pray for me."

He said that he would pray with her that she might get close to Christ. "Don't pray about anything else," he told her. They prayed several times, but still she limped. One day she told him of a wrong spirit she held in her heart against another person. She felt she should go to that person in the spirit of love, but she hesitated. Yet as she prayed that she might get close to Christ, she felt more and more that she must face up to the wrong spirit in her heart. Finally, she did the right thing, and it was not long before she was walking without a limp.

At Christmastime we long to be close to Christ. We are ashamed of our wrongs, and we are inspired to change. When we do what we should, marvelous power and peace come into our lives, and our troubles seem to vanish. We need to be close to Christ, not only at Christmas, but throughout the year. Then the joy of Christmas will continue in our hearts.

16
Who Is Jesus?

Who is Jesus? This question is naturally asked at Christmas. It is a thrilling question, for Jesus is central in all of the joyous festivities that mark His birth; His influence has kept Christmas a living, vital and deeply significant day through all the centuries. The more we know Him the more Christmas becomes an occasion for thanksgiving and adoration. To answer the question we might search through books to learn what others have said about Him. We might read from the vast treasury of poetry and literature, history and philosophy, devotion and theology. In them we should find grand and eloquent testimonies.

But let us rather just think quietly about Him. As we meditate, many pictures of Him come into focus. We see a young mother sitting by a manger in a stable. We hear a baby cry, and the cry sounds like that of all babies.

Then we picture a young man who lives in a small village. He romps with the other children. He goes to school with them. He learns to handle skillfully the tools in His father's little carpenter shop. At the age of thirty, freed now from domestic responsibilities, He walks about the countryside and preaches to those who will listen. Quietly, sometimes dramatically, always lovingly, He interprets the will of God. God is His single concern. He speaks of God's will and of God's way. He urges, persuasively and eloquently, that men must know God and acknowledge their responsibilities to their heavenly Father. The common people hear Him gladly. At times multitudes throng about Him; when people look upon Him, they sense the presence of God. In Him and through Him God becomes very real.

At times He is very lonely though He has a small circle of intimate friends and a wider circle of enthusiastic admirers. The hearts of many are inflamed with a passionate devotion, but many people turn from Him. His demands and the disciplines He requires are too great. Evil men plot His destruction.

One day we see Him tried before an unfair court on untrue charges. One of His closest friends betrays Him; the other friends flee in fear and He stands alone, courageous and faithful to God's will for His life. He is condemned to die and is nailed to a cross between thieves, leaving only the coat He has worn. The soldiers gamble for the possession of it. Through the courtesy of a friend, His body is given a decent burial.

One by one the scenes in His life come before us; it amazes us that we do know so much about Him. We know less about Caesar, who ruled the world at that time, and we know almost nothing about Pilate, the governor. We do not know who was the wealthiest man of that day, nor have we a list of the most socially prominent families.

Although nearly twenty centuries separate Him from us, our thinking about Him strangely influences us. We feel cleaner, happier, and are ashamed of our sins. We love Him, and our love for Him creates in us a love for others. Our fellowship with Him through faith compels us to affirm that never was there one like Him.

Once Jesus asked His disciples, "Who do men say that the Son of man is?" Simon Peter answered, "You are the Christ, the Son of the living God." Jesus then replied, ". . . flesh and blood has not revealed this to you, but my Father who is in heaven" (Matthew 16:13, 16, 17). We may learn about Jesus by reading books, but we learn about Christ through experience. When we know Him, we realize that He is divine; our minds and hearts embrace this truth.

Because many people know about Jesus and do not know Christ, they argue about who He is. Christian faith in Christ affirms four things about Him. First, Christ's birth was different from that of all others. An angel appeared to a pure young woman and told her that she would give birth to the Son of the Highest. She was puzzled and asked, " 'How can this be, since I have no husband?' And the angel said to her, 'The Holy Spirit will come upon you, and the power of the Most High will overshadow you; therefore the child to be born will be called holy, the Son of God' " (Luke 1:34, 35). His birth was of God, and He was divine.

Second, during His life on earth, He had supernatural power. The winds and the waves obeyed His voice. He healed every known sickness. With a small boy's lunch He was able to feed a multitude. He forgave sins. He put a song in the hearts of those who were broken in spirit; He gave hope to the discouraged; He offered strength to the weary. Nicodemus said, "Rabbi, we know that you are a teacher come from God; for no one can do these signs that you do, unless God is with him" (John 3:2). The power He imparted to men is still available to those who believe in Him.

Third, His death on the cross is our doorway into eternal life. His cross is an example of sacrifice and a revelation of God's love, but it is much, much more. That Friday He did something that forever makes different our relationship to God. For the disciples it was "Black Friday"; their leader had been crucified. God, they must surely have felt, had abandoned His own. But later those disciples realized, as St. Paul testified, that ". . . God was in Christ reconciling the world to himself . . ." (2 Corinthians 5:19). When men realized that, they saw the cross, not as God's desertion of man, but as His saving power. Then "Black Friday" became "Good Friday."

Fourth, Christ rose from the dead, and His resurrection is our assurance that beyond the grave we, too, shall live. He said, ". . . because I live, you will live also" (John 14:19). Through Christ we learn the power of endless life. So, because of who Christ is, we gladly commit our lives to Him.

No one questions that a man named Jesus once lived in Galilee. Most of us are familiar with the life He lived, and His words are on the lips of multitudes. When we learn of Him, we love Him.

> If Jesus Christ is a man—
> And only a man—I say
> That of all mankind I cleave to him,
> And to him will I cleave alway.

As we read of Him, even in the cold type of the printed Gospels, we begin to feel a closeness to Him, and His life exerts a strange power over us. We know that He was more than a man. So we add Christ to Jesus. Christ means Messiah, God's anointed. Hosts of people affirm:

> If Jesus Christ is a God—
> And the only God—I swear
> I will follow him through heaven and hell,
> The earth, the sea, the air!
> > RICHARD WATSON GILDER

The strongest evidence that Jesus is the Christ, the Son of God come to earth with power to save men, is not found in the story of His life nor in His words. Rather it is found through what He does for men today. Millions of lives have been transformed by His influence, and in them He lives.

> Whatever else be lost among the years,
> Let us keep Christmas still a shining thing:
> Whatever doubts assail us, or what fears,
> Let us hold close one day, remembering
> Its poignant meaning for the hearts of men.
> Let us get back our childlike faith again.
> > GRACE NOLL CROWELL

Candle, Star, and Christmas Tree

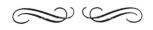

17

The Wreath of Victory

The Advent wreath, which we customarily see on the doors of homes or above the altars in our churches and which we hang with gentle care from the mantels in our living rooms, is a contribution from the Lutherans of Germany. Back in the sixteenth century, branches of fir or spruce were intertwined in a circular shape and then laid on tables in homes. On the first Sunday in Advent an upright red candle was attached to the wreath. On each succeeding Sunday another candle was added. Week by week, as the light from the burning tapers became brighter, the family was reminded by these living flames of the approach of the day of Christ's birth.

To have such a wreath on the table about which we gather each day for family prayers and devotions would not only revitalize a meaningful custom but would also become a splendid stimulus to that kind of heart preparation which gives a deeper beauty to Christmas.

We do not know why our spiritual forebears began the custom of making Advent wreaths, but we do know that the circular shape of the wreath has long symbolized both the love of God, which is without beginning or ending, and the eternal joys of heaven.

In pre-Christian times, a green laurel crown designated victory in athletic competitions and in military struggles. Such worldly achievements seemed to be shallow and temporary honors to the early Christians. These followers of Christ began the practice of placing laurel boughs on their doorposts to symbolize the greater and more enduring victory of Christ over the powers of darkness and death. Their laurel branches were often displayed during both Advent and Lent to commemorate the Lord's birth and resurrection.

The chord of joyous triumph which the Christian Church sounded could be heard above all lesser claims of victory. When the Christians assembled together they offered prayers of thanksgiving for the glories Christ had won in His resurrection. For His was no fleeting triumph; it was an accomplishment possessing eternal promise. When they prayed in Christ's name, those Christians felt that Christ's victory was something which they by faith could possess for themselves. "Now thanks be unto God," exclaimed the Apostle, "which always causeth us to triumph in Christ . . ." (2 Corinthians 2:14). "In all these things we are more than conquerors through him that loved us" (Romans 8:37). The seer of Patmos wrote, ". . . be thou faithful unto death, and I will give thee a crown of life" (Revelation 2:10).

Does it not seem strange that those early followers of Christ should have felt the spirit of victory surging through their lives? They had, it might seem to us, every reason to be full of anxiety and despair. Their Lord had been slain on a cross, their members were being persecuted, and their faithfulness was being severely tested at every turn. Yet the dominant note in the prayers they offered and in the psalms they sang was of inevitable triumph. They knew that their lives were identified through the love of Christ with the eternal purposes of Almighty God. Even the gates of hell would not long stand strong against their petitions!

Has this sense of victory become in our hearts and worshiping a diminished thing? We are so fearful and so anxious. Can we once more believe, as the early Christians believed, in the triumph of the Eternal? The wreaths on our doors at Christmas should remind us that the crown of life was won for us by Christ in His victory over sin and death.

18

Candles of the Lord

One of the oldest of all Christian symbols and surely the one that is second only to the cross in the richness of its many meanings is the burning candle or taper. Long before Christians began to celebrate Christmas as the day of our Lord's birth, the candle was used to signify Christ as the Light of the world.

The spiritual association of light with God is of ancient origin. God is the father of light: "And God said, Let there be light: and there was light. And God saw the light, that it was good: and God divided the light from the darkness" (Genesis 1:3–4). The psalmist, who exclaimed, ". . . in thy light shall we see light" (36:9), prayed also that we may ". . . walk, O Lord, in the light of thy countenance" (89:15). The words that God speaks are words of light, and His Word is a light unto the paths of men and a lamp unto their feet. A pillar of light guided the wandering feet of the Children of Israel through the wilderness, and God has provided light for the journeyings of men ever since.

When the prophet of old spoke of the coming Messiah, he used the language of light: "The people that walked in darkness have seen a great light: they that

74

dwell in the land of the shadow of death, upon them hath the light shined" (Isaiah 9:2). The One of whom he spoke is Christ, the Light-bringer and Light-giver, who is Himself ". . . the true Light, which lighteth every man that cometh into the world" (John 1:9). St. Paul testified: ". . . God, who commanded light to shine out of darkness, hath shined in our hearts, to give the light of the knowledge of the glory of God in the face of Christ Jesus" (2 Corinthians 4:6).

In the Scriptures light means goodness, truth, life, love, and wisdom; darkness is all that is in contrast, including ignorance, sin, and death.

Because Christ is the Light of all lights, we naturally associate candles particularly with Christmas. Large glowing candles, beautiful red tapers, twinkling and radiant electric candles are in the windows of stores and homes, on the branches of Christmas trees, at the center of our banquet tables, and on the altars in our churches. Always these candles should be silent witnesses to that glorious light of Bethlehem.

In medieval times a wonderful story was related that on Christmas Eve the Christ Child wanders throughout the world, looking always for places where He will be welcomed. Those who loved Him, hoping that He might find their homes, placed lighted candles in their windows.

No one, of course, could possibly know in what guise the Child might appear. Perhaps He would come dressed in the rags of a beggar, or He might come as a poor and lonely child. So it became customary for devout persons to welcome into their homes all who knocked at their doors on Christmas Eve. To turn any away may have meant the rejection of the Child, who had come in an unfamiliar garb.

Such an attitude of charitable benevolence seems especially appropriate at the time of year when we remember God's good and gracious gift, His Son, who taught us that ". . . Inasmuch as ye have done it unto one of the least of these my brethren, ye have done it unto me" (Matthew 25:40).

No longer do we believe that the Christ Child is wandering along our streets looking for homes where He will be given warmth and a welcome. Yet does not a candle at our window suggest to our neighbors and friends that He is our Guest and that there is room in our hearts for Him?

But these ideas do not by any means exhaust the rich meanings of the Christmas candle. The candle also represents loyal discipleship. Jesus, who called Himself the Light of the world, also told His friends that they, too, were to be lights in the world. St. Paul admonished, ". . . in the midst of a crooked and perverse nation . . . ye shine as lights in the world" (Philippians 2:15). Jesus told this parable: "Neither do men light a candle, and put it under a bushel, but on a candlestick; and it giveth light unto all that are in the house" (Matthew 5:15). When our lives radiate the spirit of Christ's loving compassion, we become, as the ancient poet said, "candles of the Lord" (Proverbs 20:27).

Christians are the candles by which the world is made bright with hope and spiritual confidence. A candle must be lighted from another's torch. The flame by which we burn is Christ. There is for Christians no other source of light. An inscription for a Christmas candle by Anna Hempstead Branch reads:

> As in the Holy Christ Child's name
> This blessed wax shall feed the flame—
> So let my heart its fires begin
> And light the Heavenly Pilgrim in.

The candle suggests two things about our Christian discipleship. The first is that a burning candle, while it is giving light, is being consumed. Does this not say something worth remembering about Christ? He came to give us life, but He also "laid down his life for us" (1 John 3:16). Two verses from Second Corinthians seem particularly relevant: "Though he was rich, yet for your sakes he became poor, that ye through his poverty might be rich" (8:9) and "He died for all, that they which live should not henceforth live unto themselves, but unto him which died for them" (5:15).

The life of each Christian, like that of his Master, ought to be self-giving and self-sacrificing. Christ expects that we shall willingly surrender ourselves in deeds of loving helpfulness for others. Our gifts may seem small, but even a cup of cold water, when offered in love, will comfort parched lips and quicken cold hearts.

> O Little Child of Bethlehem,
>   Why do your young eyes grieve?
> What do your outstretched arms implore
>   Of us this Christmas Eve?

"Look! In the dark streets shineth
  No Everlasting Light,
Hearts, crucified by daily fears,
  Watch through the silent night.

"Their arms hold tight to little ones,
  Tear-blinded eyes turn East,
Too tired to ask for more than crumbs,
  Dropped from My Christmas Feast."

O Little Child of Bethlehem,
  Descend to us, we pray,
And show our hearts how best to share
  With these, on Christmas Day.

If a candle in the window were truly to signify our willingness to become servants of humanity, giving light even as we ourselves are being consumed, then no child of man would wander on our streets at Christmas.

The second suggestion which the candle offers concerning our Christian discipleship is that, although one candle may not shed much light, many candles will brightly illumine any dark place. This speaks of our need for Christian fellowship. One candle—the witness of an individual Christian—seems small indeed, but it does represent one point wherein the darkness is pierced by light. We should, as the gospel hymn says, brighten the corner where we are. Many Christians, each accepting his responsibility as a follower of Christ, will lift whatever darkness of doubt, despair, or fear that shrouds our world. Then there will indeed be such a light that nothing shall extinguish!

> Blow cold against the flame,
> Throw sand upon the spark;
> You cannot keep the Light
> From shining in the dark.

19

The Star in the East

Many plants and flowers are featured in our remembrance of Christ's nativity. An ancient tale relates that at the hour of our Lord's birth the trees in the forests burst into bloom and the birds began to sing. Among the most familiar Christmas greenery are the mistletoe, the holly, evergreen trees, and ivy. Flowers which have in various places in Christendom been associated with this season are cherry blossoms, rosemary, and the Christmas rose.

The favorite Christmas plant is the poinsettia, whose gorgeous red bracts or leaves surround an almost inconspicuous yellow flower. The normal period of maturity of poinsettias is in midwinter, and so they flourish at a season when their colors of bright red and green seem especially appropriate.

Poinsettias are named for the Hon. Joel Roberts Poinsett, onetime congressman and a member of President Van Buren's Cabinet. He served for a time as our minister to Mexico. While he represented the American people in Mexico, he continued his great interests in plants and flowers. He was especially attracted to the flaming leaves of poinsettias, a plant which grows in profusion in both Mexico and Central America.

When Mr. Poinsett returned to his home in South Carolina, he spent much time trying to cultivate these beautiful plants in a strange climate. His careful efforts were rewarded, and his achievement has given us one of our most beloved Christmas flowers.

Not much is now remembered concerning Mr. Poinsett's long political career, but we may feel certain that his continuing love of flowers indicates that he was a man who loved all of God's marvelous creations. His gift to us of the poinsettia surely is as splendid and as inspiring a contribution to our Christmas celebrations as the gifts of music and art from other men whose minds were also dedicated to the Babe of Bethlehem.

The poinsettia is a plant of exquisite beauty. It also symbolizes for many of us the shining star that led the steps of the Wise Men. This association of the fiery leaves of the poinsettia with the star of Bethlehem makes it an especially meaningful adornment for our churches and homes.

As the Magi of old were guided along strange roads to the crib of our Lord, so have Christians of every generation been directed through their pilgrimages in life. The hand of the Eternal may bring us to green pastures and still waters, and beyond to the valleys of many shadows, for always "the steps of a good man are ordered by the Lord . . ." (Psalms 37:23).

Stars speak of other worlds. Their radiance comes from afar. They testify to a realm beyond our earth. Christmas, too, has just such a message for each of us. Above our busy lives, high over our many activities, and above our doubts and fears, there is a Spirit which

presides and counsels, plans and guides. Above us all
is God in whom we move and have our being.

Stars are constant and dependable. They bring to
our thoughts this additional spiritual truth: God is
eternal and steadfast. Astronomers can predict with
accuracy the movements of stars. They can tell what
were the positions of particular stars thousands of
years ago, and they can foretell their movements for
thousands of years into the future. Our human lives
are fickle; our steps turn at the slightest whim; our
plans are altered by the weakest arguments. How
good it is to know that God is the same yesterday,
today, and forever! Like the stars high in His heavens,
God challenges our inconstancy by His dependability.

Stars also shine most clearly at night. When the
earth is darkest, the stars are brightest. Stars remind us
that when we are overwhelmed by clouds of despondency and when our lives are shrouded in nights of
fear, then we see most clearly the light of God's truth
and the brightness of His all-comprehending love.

The Wise Men followed the star, and they found the
Christ. They were not sure of their destination. But
they believed the star, for to them the star represented
God's guiding hand. And their faith was rewarded.
The star of Bethlehem was high above the heads of all
men, but only the Wise Men followed it. In their
hearts there was confidence. Faith in the heart is prerequisite for all star-led journeys. If we believe in
God, He will lead us. When we trust Him, He will
show us the way to Christ.

Zacharias prophesied of the Christ Child: ". . . the

dayspring from on high hath visited us, To give light to them that sit in darkness and in the shadow of death, to guide our feet into the way of peace" (Luke 1:78–79). Jesus is "the bright and morning star" (Revelation 22:16), and in Him we may find our bearings through life and eternity.

Nancy Byrd Turner has captured the deeper meanings of the poinsettia symbol in these words:

> High in the heavens a single star,
>   Of pure, imperishable light;
> Out on the desert strange and far
>   Dim riders riding through the night:
> Above a hilltop sudden song
>   Like silver trumpets down the sky—
> And all to welcome One so young
>   He scarce could lift a cry!
>
> Stars rise and set, that star shines on:
>   Songs fail, but still that music beats
> Through all the ages come and gone,
>   In land and field and city streets.
> And we who catch the Christmas gleam,
>   Watching with children on the hill,
> We know, we know it is no dream—
>   He stands among us still!

20

Tree of Life

On a clear winter night more than four hundred years ago, Martin Luther was walking toward his home. As his feet followed familiar paths, his eyes gazed upon the radiant beauty of the heavens which were declaring the glory of the Lord. Looking through the branches of the evergreens, he saw far beyond the hundreds of stars that seemed to be sprinkled on the sky like golden jewels. He may well have recalled the words of the ancient chronicler: "Then shall the trees of the wood sing out at the presence of the Lord . . ." (1 Chronicles 16:33).

So enthralled was Luther that he wished that he might somehow preserve and share with his loved ones the evening's matchless splendor. If he could only take one of those trees into his home, how greatly would his family rejoice in its beauty! So it was, legend tells us, that Luther took a small tree into his home on Christmas Eve. On its branches he placed lighted candles so that both young and old might know something of the beauty of stars shining through the branches of trees.

Whether this was the first Christmas tree no one can for certain say, but we do know that some five or six decades later the custom of bringing trees into the home at Christmas was well established in Strasbourg. This most delightful of our Christmas traditions spread rapidly to the homes of people living along the Rhine and Danube rivers and then to many other parts of Europe.

In the latter years of the seventeenth century, German immigrants brought the custom to their new American homes in western Pennsylvania. Later German immigrants, who settled elsewhere in colonial America, also introduced Christmas trees. We can imagine how their neighbors eagerly adopted the practice, incorporating the tree into the traditional observances which mirrored their own national origins.

In 1776, when Hessian soldiers were waging the struggle of George III against the colonists, some of these men, remembering their native Christmas celebrations, set up trees at Trenton. On Christmas night of that year General Washington made his storied crossing of the Delaware River and achieved a decisive victory over the British garrison, who were slumbering after having observed the holy night in the wrong ways.

In the middle of the nineteenth century, Albert of Saxony, the husband of Queen Victoria, shared the German enthusiasm for Christmas trees with the English people by having one set up in Windsor Castle. Christmas trees soon became a favorite holiday feature throughout the British Isles.

The Christmas tree is not found among all Christian peoples, but it is surely the most common tradition throughout most of the world. Even in the southern hemisphere, where December days are among the warmest in the year, the tree and its burden of tinsel and artificial icicles is common.

Nowadays Americans harvest more than thirty million trees annually for use during the Christmas season. That home in which a spruce or fir, a pine or a red cedar or arborvitae is not decorated is rare indeed. At the top of most trees is placed the star of Bethlehem as a silent reminder of the night of our Lord's birth and perhaps as a testimony to the wonder that filled the heart of Martin Luther.

Many of us look beyond the tree itself to those silent testimonies concerning the meanings of the Christian faith. Some of us have spent the Christmas season in places where the bare limbs of trees stand in bold relief against a white wilderness of snow. As our eyes have surveyed the landscape, we have been delighted to see evergreens whose greenness is accentuated against the white background.

Just such a contrast between the apparent life of the evergreen and the apparent death of the other trees was long ago suggested to our European ancestors. The evergreens' perennial greenness symbolized to them both length of days and life eternal. Evergreens represented to them the resurrection and immortality.

Such spiritual associations with evergreens are not now frequently remembered, yet when we think deeply about the meanings of Christmas, we can readily see that the tree is much more than something on which to hang glass balls and plastic ornaments. The tree is a wonderful interpreter of certain fundamental truths that are to be found in the words of Him who came that we through Him might have eternal life.

Many generations of faithful Christians have believed the tree to represent the *lignum vitae,* the tree of life of which Old Testament writers spoke.

There are not many carols about the Christmas tree, but one old German melody does acclaim the spiritual message to which we have alluded.

O Christmas tree! Fair Christmas tree!
A type of life eternal!
O Christmas tree! Fair Christmas tree!
Your boughs are ever vernal.
So fresh and green in summer heat,
And bright when snows lie round your feet.
O Christmas tree! Fair Christmas tree!
A type of life eternal!

O Christmas tree! Fair Christmas tree!
You tell the timeless story.
O Christmas tree! Fair Christmas tree!
You speak of Jesus' glory.
With gifts of love and songs of mirth,
With tidings of our Saviour's birth.
O Christmas tree! Fair Christmas tree!
You tell the timeless story.

O Christmas tree! Fair Christmas tree!
Alight with love and splendor;
O Christmas tree! Fair Christmas tree!
True praise to Christ you render;
In steadfast faith you flash with light,
As stars of God glow through the night.
O Christmas tree! Fair Christmas tree!
Alight with love and splendor.

Nothing so brings to our hearts the buoyant Christmas joy as Christ's assurance that one day we shall rise on the wings of faith to dwell forever in the presence of God. The tree in our homes may become the means by which we not only rediscover meanings which undergirded the Christian faith of our forefathers but the means too by which we shall anticipate that most joyous of all festivals, when, beneath the Tree of Life, we shall look upon Him whom we have seen before in only a dim and reflected glory.

21

Story of the Gift-Bringer

In 1822, Dr. Clement Clarke Moore, a distinguished professor at the General Theological Seminary of New York, wrote a ballad which he called, "Visit from St. Nicholas." These verses, which were written only for the amusement of his own children, were later printed without Dr. Moore's permission. Ever since they have been closely identified with the popular figure of Santa Claus. Dr. Moore, who was a Hebrew scholar and the son of a man who served both as rector of Trinity Church in New York and as president of Columbia University, did not put much stock in his poetic creation, for it was not until 1838, when the poem had become widely popular, that he claimed credit publicly for the familiar lines.

Dr. Moore had unwittingly given small children everywhere their most vivid picture of Santa Claus and his reindeer. When we think of Christmas we invariably associate the day with the plump, jolly, white-bearded man who was created in Dr. Moore's ingenious imagination.

Yet the story of the gift-bringer—his name and personality differ with time and circumstance—is as old as Christmas. God was the first gift-giver. John 3:16

reads: "For God so loved the world, that he gave his only begotten Son, that whosoever believeth in him should not perish, but have everlasting life." St. Matthew tells us that the Magi came from the East to Bethlehem bearing gorgeous gifts for the Baby Jesus, whom they worshiped as their newly born king.

In some lands it is the Christ Child who is believed to distribute gifts and blessings, although the name Kris Kringle, a popular variation of the German word "Christkindel"—which means "Christ Child"—is now commonly associated with Santa Claus.

The real prototype of the modern Santa was a fourth-century bishop of Myra in Asia Minor, St. Nicholas. Little historical information concerning him has been preserved, yet about his name has clung a wonderful world of lore and tradition. Legend tells us that he was a young man of considerable wealth who gave himself to the work of the Lord and generously bestowed his worldly goods upon those whose needs were greater than his own. Usually he preferred to receive no credit for his benevolences, desiring rather to make his visits to the homes of the poor and unfortunate under the cloak of darkness so that no one would know who he was.

This venerated man, we are further told, suffered tortures and imprisonment when the Emperor Diocletian was striving ruthlessly to destroy the Christian faith. During the reign of the Christian emperor, Constantine the Great, St. Nicholas was released, and he later is said to have attended the important Council of Nicaea.

St. Nicholas has long been associated particularly

with the interests of scholars, mariners, and especially children. He is the patron saint of Greece and Russia. Centuries ago, December 6 was designated as the day when he should be honored. The proximity of his day to the birthday of our Lord made him an obvious representative of the charitable character of Christmas. In colonial America the Dutch name Sant Nikolaas was mispronounced as Santa Claus. It is by this name that St. Nicholas is best remembered.

Do you believe in Santa Claus? Many people have serious doubts about the propriety of passing on to their children the wonderful stories concerning the jolly bringer of Yuletide cheer.

Questions about Santa Claus are not new. In the last years of the nineteenth century there was a bewildered little girl named Virginia O'Hanlon who wasn't herself quite sure. So she wrote a letter to the New York *Sun*. She was certain that the people of that newspaper knew just about everything, and she felt that anything they might tell her would be altogether right.

Francis P. Church wrote the famous answer to Virginia's query. In simple and unaffected words he told her of his own belief in Santa Claus: "He exists as certainly as love and generosity and devotion exist, and you know that they abound and give to your life its highest beauty and joy. Alas! how dreary would be the world if there was no Santa Claus!"

Mr. Church's answer apparently confirmed the wavering belief of eight-year-old Virginia, and has given confidence to children—and to their parents—ever since.

Now there are certainly some kinds of Santas whom we cannot believe in. We disbelieve in a Santa who browbeats little children into good behavior on the pretext that he will avoid their stockings if they aren't the highly improbable little cherubs their mothers think they should be. And we have misgivings about Santas who smoke big cigars, use profane words, or try their best to drink more than anyone else at office parties. And that Santa is an impostor who so completely identifies himself with Christmas that he pushes from our minds the little Child of Bethlehem whose name this season should reverence. Better no Santa Claus at all than frauds like these who defame and spiritually impoverish the Lord's birthday!

But we can surely believe that much that is most precious in Christmas may be symbolized in the cheerful benevolence of the jolly and friendly person who has no other purpose in life than that of spreading joy and communicating to young and old the gracious meanings of goodwill. We anticipate the sound of his sleigh bells at our school and church parties. We see him standing day after day near the Salvation Army sign at the street corner. On Christmas Eve he enters our homes during the wee hours in order that, later on, the eyes of small children may shine like silver dollars. Santa does deeds of kind thoughtfulness which can be done by no one else in just the same way.

Even in our society, where we often have difficulty finding gifts for "the man who has everything" and in which many gifts are labeled merely as "conversation pieces," the giving and receiving of gifts at Christmas seems to be the most normal and natural way we have of expressing our genuine sense of joyfulness.

Yet Christmas giving should not be limited to an exchange of gifts. We come closer to the spirit of the Christian Christmas when we think of others and not primarily of what we shall receive in return. At Christmas, perhaps more than at any other season, there should be an outgoing spirit of goodwill. When our attitude is like that of Santa Claus and we give no thought to what we shall get, then we come closer to the spirit of our Saviour who gave completely and never counted the cost.

22

The Sprig of Healing

This is a scene that has been enacted in many homes. Late one afternoon, shortly before Christmas, Father brings home a curious little package. Mother and the children look quizzically at each other. At this time of year, when everyone has the privilege of keeping secrets, no one ventures to ask the inevitable question, "What is it?" Father's eyes gleam brightly and soon he can no longer suppress his grin.

Then one of the children exclaims, "Mistletoe!" Immediately the family moves into action. Each one knows from previous years what his particular chore is. The son goes for the stepladder, the daughter hurries to the garage for the hammer, and the mother's skilled fingers transform an ordinary ribbon into a matchless bow. Soon one sprig of mistletoe is hanging above the door and another is fastened securely to the chandelier in the living room. Now everyone feels that the home is properly dressed up for the holidays.

A bit of mistletoe, however small, adds a measure of joy that is all out of proportion to its size. Although Christians have hung mistletoe in their homes for many generations, long before the evangelization of Britain the Druids claimed that the plant possessed strange and wonderful healing powers.

The Druids were pre-Christian Celtic priests. The

harvesting of mistletoe was for them a ritual that was attended with much solemnity and fanfare. Dressed in white ceremonial robes, the priests mounted the trees and cut the mistletoe branches with golden sickles.

Belief in the medicinal benefits of mistletoe has long since perished, along with the peculiar rites and rituals of the Druids. But for Christians, the sprigs of mistletoe came to represent the One of whom the Druids were unaware, Christ the Healer.

Christmas brings into our homes and hearts a beneficent and healing spirit. It is good to have mistletoe as a quiet reminder of Him of whom we sing:

> Light and life to all He brings,
> Risen with healing in His wings.

Long ago in Palestine the touch of the hand of Christ brought sight to darkened eyes and health to weary limbs. Henry Twells describes the Master's healing ministry in the words of his familiar hymn:

> At even, when the sun was set,
> The sick, O Lord, around Thee lay;
> O in what divers pains they met!
> O with what joy they went away!

The miracles Christ wrought in Galilee may be realized in our lives at this season, if we turn to Him in trust and faith. As He bound up the brokenhearted, offered a healing balm for sick souls, and brought light to blinded minds, so does He minister even now to weary mariners on life's tempestuous seas.

". . . blessed are they that have not seen, and yet have believed" (John 20:29), for to them at Christmas will come a soul-restoring and spirit-quickening gift of life.

There is, of course, no healing virtue in a sprig of mistletoe, yet it symbolizes for us the health, and vigor, and joy that came into the world through the life-enhancing blessings of the Great Physician.

But most of us associate mistletoe more generally with the delightful custom of kissing under the hanging bough. The practice of kissing anyone who unwittingly—or wittingly!—stands under the mistletoe is of English origin and is centuries old. When in ancient times two warriors happened to meet each other under a tree to which mistletoe had attached itself, they immediately dropped their weapons and embraced. Some magical spell was apparently caused by the presence of mistletoe. Would that such a spell might fall upon those who sit in the councils of nations at this season!

From this old belief men came to feel that at Christmastime the hearts of all men should be bound by love and goodwill. When in olden times a young man kissed a fair young maiden under the mistletoe, he silently pledged to her his life and love. In no other situation was their love so eloquently expressed. That is a far cry, isn't it, from the kind of promiscuous kissing under the mistletoe that is accomplished in our homes by the young gallants! Yet mistletoe may well become for us a testimony of the peace and love which are so closely embroidered in the fabric of this season.

The early Christians, when they met for worship,

sealed their love for one another with "a holy kiss." In a way you might say that every kiss, meaningfully offered and graciously accepted, has a certain holiness. It is always a pledge and a promise of devotion and selfless affection.

Recently a judge, when counselling with a young couple who were asking for a divorce, suggested that they "kiss and make up." "Here and now?" the young man asked incredulously. "Yes, here and now," said the judge. "Do you know of a better time or place?" Well, the young man did kiss his wife, and their hard and drawn faces softened once more and their long pent-up love for each other was no longer withheld. Then the judge said something which might not be expected to be heard in judicial chambers: "The trouble with too many young married couples is that they don't express their love often enough."

If there is to be peace among the nations and among the races of men, it will have to come through homes where patterns of harmony have replaced notes of discord. When two persons drop their weapons of pride, stubbornness, and conceit, and embrace under the mistletoe, it would seem that the healing hands of Christ are laid upon their heads in a divine benediction.

23

Greeting of Blessedness

None of us could possibly imagine the number of times during these last few days that we have greeted friends with the words "Merry Christmas." No other greeting seems quite as appropriate; anything less than these words would indicate that the spirit of Christmas has passed indifferently by.

The words "Merry Christmas" ought not to be said casually, or only for want of something else to say. These words, which have been exchanged at this season for centuries, seem to me to represent more the mood of a prayer than of an offhand salutation.

Our word "merry" generally suggests mirth, gaiety, and jollity. It bespeaks fellowship, high spirits, and lightheartedness. All of these are a part of the wish we extend to our friends. But centuries ago the word "merry" had other meanings and connotations. "Merry" meant peacefulness and blessedness. It was as though one were saying, "A peaceful Christmas to you" or "May Christmas bring the blessings of God to you."

A familiar and beloved eighteenth-century carol expresses this idea of peace and blessing. Notice the punctuation in the first line:

God rest you merry, gentlemen,
Let nothing you dismay,
Remember Christ our Saviour
Was born on Christmas Day.

Maybe we need both meanings, the old and the new. But mostly, when we say "Merry Christmas" we are hoping that the spiritual peace of God may rest upon the lives and homes of our friends, and that through such a blessing they may find real joy and release from life's hardships and heartaches. "Merry Christmas" is a prayer for divine benediction.

No matter how crowded the gaily wrapped packages may be around the trees in our homes, I am sure any of us would willingly surrender all of them for the gifts of peace of mind and quietness of soul. No friend, however generous, can give you these gifts, and yet they are available to any man who has faith in his heart. God, who gave His Son that we through Him might have fullness of life, will give to each of us His peace that passeth all understanding and His blessing which is an unspeakable gift. These gifts are denied to no man, whether he be young or old, strong or weak, rich or poor. "Desire spiritual gifts," wrote St. Paul.

Soon the shouting and the tumult of our preparations for Christmas will die down, the crowded stores and business streets will be emptied, fires will be lighted in our hearths, lights from candles and trees will shine brightly, carollers may sing outside our doors, many will turn for a few moments to their churches for late worship services, and then stockings will be hung and quiet will come to our homes. Something wonderful and marvelous will enter our lives if through faith we open our hearts to God's abiding peace and blessing.

Whatever Christmas means to you, and it means many things to many people, it will sound only a hollow chord if it brings not God into our lives and an awareness of Christ's presence into our hearts.

24

The Crib and the Cross

Everyone loves small children. The Christmas story centers in a birth—under strange circumstances and in a far-gone day to be sure—but of a wee Child all the same. I am sure that much of our perennial fondness for the nativity story may be explained by our natural and normal love of all that attends the entry into our world of a new child.

But the nativity story gives only the first few fleeting impressions, lovingly preserved and skillfully related by the evangelists Matthew and Luke, of the greatest life ever lived. During thirty-three swiftly moving years our Lord ministered to human need, taught the eager hearts of multitudes of men of the eternal love of their heavenly Father, and then gave His life on a cross that those who love and believe in Him might be reconciled to God. What a very small portion of His magnificent life is revealed in those scenes where Mary and Joseph greet the bright-eyed shepherds and welcome the Wise Men who have come from far beyond the horizon!

Five miles beyond Bethlehem, where loving hands gently laid the Child in a manger, lies Jerusalem, where cruel hands hurled the body of the Saviour upon a cross. On a clear day a traveler may look from Bethlehem to the heights of Jerusalem. At this season each of us should acquire that perspective. As we stand by the crib our eyes should be uplifted to His cross. Dr. Frederick Keller Stamm has penned these telling words:

> This is a different Jesus from the one about whom we sing our time-honored Christmas carols. We can cuddle the Babe, grow sentimental about Him, and pity the mother who had to give birth to Him in a cow stable. *But He grew up*, and the Church has on its hands a mature Man who makes stern demands, disturbs its smugness, and asks us to rearrange our lives so that we can take up a cross and follow Him. No one thinks ill of a church that is kind to a Baby, honors Him with a beautifully lighted creche on the church lawn, and remains itself in the infant stage of Christianity. It gets itself crucified and rises to maturity of life only when it walks the Golgotha slope with a Man whose alleged madness is the only cure for an insane world.

I wonder how many people have no knowledge of Christ beyond the beautiful stories of His birth? Surely those who know little more than that angels pierced the silence of a dark night with a song of heaven-sent peace have missed the whole point of His life! In His incarnation Jesus shares the character of all mortals, but only that God through Him might communicate His divine will to the children of men. That will was portrayed on the canvas of Calvary.

Wouldn't it be wonderful if, in the midst of our joyous Christmas festivities, there were some symbol or token which would remind us that the Baby grew up? Long ago faithful men in northern Europe brought into their churches and homes an appropriate reminder that Jesus on His cross became the world's Saviour. That reminder was branches from great holly trees. The sharp points on the evergreen leaves became for them symbols of the crown of thorns which was pressed upon the head of our Lord on the day of His crucifixion, and the bright red berries were representative of His blood which was shed for the remission of sin.

The spiritual significance of our Christmas holly was captured generations ago in the words of this traditional English carol:

> The holly and the ivy,
>   Now both are full well grown,
> Of all the trees that are in the wood,
>   The holly bears the crown.
>
> The holly bears a blossom
>   As white as lily flower;
> Mary bore sweet Jesus Christ,
>   To be our sweet Saviour.
>
> The holly bears a berry,
>   As red as any blood;
> And Mary bore sweet Jesus Christ,
>   To do poor sinners good.

The holly bears a prickle,
  As sharp as any thorn;
And Mary bore sweet Jesus Christ,
  On Christmas Day in the morn.

The holly bears a bark,
  As bitter as any gall;
And Mary bore sweet Jesus Christ,
  For to redeem us all.

The holly and the ivy,
  Now both are full well grown,
Of all the trees that are in the wood,
  The holly bears the crown.

The eagerness with which many Americans have thoughtlessly, almost ruthlessly, gathered holly to decorate their homes threatens soon to make holly trees extinct in some parts of our nation. Yet the holly branch has become one of our most common designs for greeting cards, wrapping paper, and seals. Lest Christmas become a matter only of such superficials, we would do well to appreciate, as did our fathers before us, that holly calls to mind our Master's willing surrender of Himself on a cross that all men through Him might be saved.

The sentiment and the beauty of the Christmas story is the prologue to the far grander story of human redemption. The span of days between Christmas and Easter is, like the miles between Bethlehem and Jerusalem, very brief, but in those two hallowed days is mirrored the full life of Him through whom we claim abundant life.

25

Cards of Greeting

Every generation adds some new custom or practice to the legacy of Christmas observances. The most recent of the popular Christmas customs is the sending of greeting cards. Millions of cards now pass through the post offices during December. The average American family sends—and receives—more than sixty.

A business executive claims that twenty thousand cards, each bearing his name, are mailed annually and that his lists grow by several thousand names each year. Most of us, however, wish only to send a few well-chosen cards to a few well-beloved friends. We have no particular desire to pile high the cards we receive in order to impress our friends or to encourage our own sense of importance.

Christmas greeting cards were introduced in England in the 1840s. They are said to have been preceded by the elaborately drawn and eloquently worded greetings which schoolboys, away from home during the holidays, prepared for their parents as expressions of love and incidentally as evidences of the proficiency they had acquired in the second "R"— 'riting.

By the 1870s, when the sending of cards was a widely accepted practice in England, the custom was introduced in America. None of the enterprising printers of that day could have imagined what future their efforts would bring! Today one can secure, as early as July, cards of any kind or description and suitable for any temperament or disposition.

Some hand-weary addressers of Christmas cards probably feel that this is one good custom—to paraphrase Tennyson—that seems likely to corrupt the world. Sometimes, as we lay down our pens, we wonder if we have not, willy-nilly, become dupes and slaves to custom.

But this wonderful custom does not need unduly to tire or depress us. It can be, and indeed for many people is, the most thoughtful way of keeping in touch with old friends and also is a sincere way of expressing and sharing Christmas wishes.

How can this highly commercialized custom be spiritualized so that it deepens, rather than exhausts, our Christmas sentiments? First, the cards we choose may reflect the genuine spirit and meaning of Christmas. Some cards are both irrelevant and irreverent; others are ribald, saucy, and downright disgusting. Those cards which possess most appeal do not mirror shallow superficialities but rather proclaim the angels' message of peace on earth, goodwill to men.

Secondly, the cards we mail may be true witnesses of our faith in Christ, bridging to the hearts of distant friends. When signing cards we may offer brief prayers in behalf of those to whom we are writing. Sometimes we shall have the assurance that they, too, are offering petitions on the wings of their prayers.

Dr. Charles W. Eliot long ago wrote these words that are inscribed on the wall of the post office building in our nation's capital:

> Messenger of sympathy and love,
> Servant of parted friends,
> Consoler of the lonely,
> Bond of the scattered family,
> Enlarger of the common life.

If our cards are dispatched in the spirit of these words, then the exchange of greetings at Christmas will always be a delight and a blessing, and never a burdensome chore.

26

Christmas as a Bane or Blessing

Can you imagine a year without Christmas? For many years Christmas was actually ignored by devout persons and its celebration was prohibited by law.

In seventeenth-century England, at the time when the Puritans were in political ascendancy, the observance of Christmas became illegal. The markets were ordered to stay open for business as usual on Christmas Day, and violators were jailed. The law even stipulated that the preparing of fancy pies and plum puddings be banned. On December 25 church doors were locked, and no worship services were permitted.

Later, when England was once more governed by a monarch who found delight in the ancient Christmas customs, the Puritans derided these traditions and referred to the season as "Fooltide."

The Puritan influence reached to the American colonies. In 1659, a New England law attempted to bar all Christmas observances. Many Yankees did not accept the popular Christmas festivities until well into the nineteenth century.

William Bradford, a Mayflower Pilgrim and long-time governor of Plymouth Colony, penned these words in his journal in 1620:

> On ye day called Christmas-day, ye Gov'r
> called them out to work (as was usual), but ye
> most of this new company excused themselves,
> and said it went against their consciences to
> work on ye day.

The governor acceded to the people's protestations, but later, when they engaged in various sports, "he went to them and took away their implements, and told them it was against his conscience that they should play." Bradford adds this comment: "Since which time nothing hath been attempted that way, at least, openly."

What spoilsports those Puritans must have been! Yet even today, in the midst of our highly secularized Christmas observances, their reasons are worth considering. Christmas, falling on a weekday, detracted, the Puritans felt, from the significance of the Sabbath as being the particular day of the Lord. They also objected to the fact that many of the customs associated with Christmas had come from heathen origins. Especially did they frown upon the riotous and drunken behavior that had become common at Christmastime.

In our day, when frantic furor characterizes our preparations for Christmas, there are people who have suggested that perhaps the Puritans were right. Many of us have heard friends exclaim, "Not Christmas already!" Many of us have said, "I'll be glad when it is all over!" For some people Christmas means little more than the addressing of an inexhaustible number of cards, fighting through nervous and haggard crowds of people, and trying to find time to do all of the extra household chores which Christmas requires. So much time is given to wrapping presents and hanging tinsel that Christmas Day, when it comes, always seems to be an anticlimax.

We would not wish to follow the pattern of the Puritans. They went about their reforming in the wrong way. But we do need to see Christmas according to spiritual perspectives. We can, without forgoing the warm and delightful social amenities of this season, deepen our Christian understandings and appreciations of the day of Christ's nativity. "We do not as yet see everything made subject to him, but *we do see Jesus*" (Hebrews 2:8–9, Goodspeed). If He represents our central focus, Christmas will never again be a bane but always a blessing.

To sweep clean the hearth and to tidy up the house for Christmas is only a broomstick preparation. Heart preparation sweeps our lives clear of the cobwebs of indifference, the clutterings of despair and failure, and the odd accumulations of sin. Then we may claim Christmas as Christ's day and He will enter our lives as our dearest Guest. In the words of Phillips Brooks:

> No ear may hear His coming,
> But in this world of sin,
> Where meek souls will receive Him still
> The dear Christ enters in.

Christmas means many things to many people, but its meanings are superficial and transitory if they do not mean Christ. We feel that Christmas will have deeper meanings for all who seek, in the familiar traditions and customs, those intimations of Christ's divine glory.

When Christmas Came to Bethlehem

27

Christmas and Ordinary People

Is anything as common and at times more monotonous than the ordinary days of our lives? One day after another, and every one so similar. Exciting things happen to other people, but we are consigned to life's back pages. Eagerly we anticipate tomorrow, but our best-laid plans fizzle out like Roman candles. Hopefully we mix the ingredients of spunk, stamina and courage, but always some malicious Herod comes along and throws sand in the soup. We bravely read Shakespeare's noble words:

> There's a divinity that shapes our ends,
> Rough-hew them how we will.

But that's not for us. Heroically we gird for battle, but alas, we cannot move in Saul's armor. Our fate is that of Robert Frost's hired man:

> Nothing to look backward to with pride,
> And nothing to look forward to with hope.

Then comes Christmas. Christmas is our day. Christmas is for ordinary folks. Now once again we hear the beat of a distant drummer. Now we hitch all of our hopes to a shining star.

That is how it was when Christmas first came to Bethlehem. Even the setting of the nativity was commonplace. A sequestered town astride a limestone ridge, where once Jacob gently laid to rest his beloved Rachel, where Boaz claimed Ruth as his bride, and where the prophet Samuel anointed the head of the shepherd lad, David—but now, overshadowed by the splendors of Jerusalem, Bethlehem, "little among the thousands of Judah" (Micah 5:2), is a spent candle.

Two weary travelers enter the village on a night that can scarcely be distinguished from a thousand other nights. Bureaucracy must have more tax moneys! And a Child is born. A Child. Not Athena sprung fully grown and fully armored from the head of Zeus. Not a resplendent king descending in a flaming chariot from the heavens. Only a birth, the most common of human experiences. This is how God comes.

One would have expected the burst of a meteor, a brilliant sun at midnight, a burning bush, a pillar and a cloud, a parting of the waters. But none of these things happens. A Child is born at the hour of twelve, so pious legend tells us, to a mother of humble origin. We should have thought God would have chosen dawn when the heavens are aglow with the variegated colors of the rising sun, or twilight when the hand of day reaches high to pull down the purple curtains of the night. How strange are the ways of God!

Yet the very ordinariness of that first Christmas pleads knowingly and persuasively to common people. Christmas came to little Bethlehem that we might know that no place is unknown to God; at the stroke of twelve to remind us that there is no moment of the day or night when He is absent from us; to young Mary to convince us that all life is dear to Him; and in a Child that we may sense all of life is in His hands. Christmas is His monogram, stenciled on our hearts, recalling to us year by year that "no more is God a Stranger."

Christmas is person-centered. Christmas affirms that human lives—"even the least of these," like Mary, the shepherds, a Baby—are the least expendable treasures in the whole universe. W. H. Auden in *For the Time Being* says that on this day

> Everything became a You
> and nothing was an It.

The God of Bethlehem is not concerned with principles, abstractions and theories. He loves only people. He is the Good Shepherd who searches in love for even the least worthy and most neglected of the children of men.

Will Durant in *The Story of Philosophy* writes of another kind of deity:

"Aristotle's God never does anything. He has no desires, no will, no purpose. He is activity so pure that he never acts. He is absolutely perfect. Therefore He cannot desire anything . . . . His sole employment is the contemplation of himself. Poor Aristotelian God. He is a do-nothing King. The King reigns but does not rule."

Not so the God and Father of our Lord Jesus Christ.

Dr. J. B. Phillips' translation of John's Canticle of the Incarnation reads:

> At the beginning God expressed Himself. That Personal Expression was with God and was God, and He existed with God from the beginning. All creation took place through Him, and none took place without Him. In Him appeared Life and this Life was the Light of mankind. The Light still shines in the darkness, and the darkness has never put it out (John 1:1–5).

God's supreme revelation of Himself is through Personality—the Personality of Christ—so that we ordinary mortals may know and understand Him. And in the years of His ministry among men Jesus cast His lot within the vortex of human experience, linked Himself to our common human destiny, and died on a cross for such persons as you and me. Wrote John Robert Seeley in *Ecce Homo*, "He set the first and greatest example of a life wholly governed and guided by the passion of humanity."

Do you wonder that Christmas is especially precious to ordinary people? Or that on this day, more so than on any other, we think of giving, not getting, and of what we can do for others, not what they can do for us?

The nephew of Ebenezer Scrooge expresses the genuine Christmas spirit in response to his uncle's assertion that Christmas is humbug:

"I am sure I have always thought of Christmas time,

when it has come round—apart from the veneration due to its sacred name and origin, if anything belonging to it can be apart from that—as a good time; a kind, forgiving, charitable, pleasant time: the only time I know of, in the long calendar of the year, when men and women seem by one consent to open their shut-up hearts freely, and to think of people below them as if they really were fellow-passengers to the grave, and not another race of creatures bound on other journeys. And therefore, uncle, though it has never put a scrap of gold or silver in my pocket, I believe that it *has* done me good, and *will* do me good; and I say, God bless it!"

Nearly twenty centuries have come and gone since Christ's coming to Bethlehem. But even now He comes.

> Where meek souls will receive Him, still
> The dear Christ enters in.

Read prayerfully these words from the pen of Dr. Albert Schweitzer:

> He comes to us as one unknown, without a name, as of old by the lakeside he came to those men who knew him not. He speaks to us the same words, "Follow thou me," and sets us to the tasks which he has to fulfill for our time. He commands. And to those who obey, whether they be wise or simple, he will reveal himself in the toils, the conflicts, the suffering which

they shall pass through in his fellowship, and as an ineffable mystery, they shall learn in their own experience who he is.

Christmas has staked a claim on our ordinary lives, making them vessels of adoration and instruments of praise. Always this has been true. To the last syllable of recorded time this will remain true.

28

She Cradled Him in Love

Where within all history and literature may we find a more wonderful story than the nativity of Christ? This old, old story lives and glows with a new vitality each time we turn to its pages. Defying the ravages of time, the familiar words never become wearisome.

During twenty centuries men of creative genius— musicians, poets, artists, and persons possessing disciplined skills—have come under the spell of the gospel message and have dedicated such treasures of talent as no other day may claim.

Although craftsmen have adorned and embellished Christmas, human ingenuity could never have originated this story. John Sutherland Bonnell rightly exclaims, "Only God could have dreamed the Christmas story."

Why do we cling, after so many centuries, so tenaciously to the simple words recorded by the evangelists? Why does the worldwide Christian fellowship, numbering more than 900 million persons and representing every stature and degree of our common humanity, find Bethlehem to be the fountainhead of joy, inspiration and redemption?

Bethlehem surely means many things to many

people, and no genuine meaning is without significance. But towering over all, Christmas is a story of
divine and human love. Christmas is a festival of love
which has a magnetlike tug on our hearts. A compelling, compassionate and all-encompassing love ex-
plains the attractiveness of this day. Without love,
there could never have been a first Christmas. Apart
from the love we bring and the love we offer and receive, Christmas would be as dreary as an all-day
drizzle.

Central to the meaning of Christmas is the love of
our heavenly Father as interpreted and translated in
the birth of His Son. This great, undeserving and
self-giving love of God to men is at the heart of the
testimony of the early Christians.

For God so loved the world, that he gave his
only begotten Son, that whosoever believeth in
him should not perish, but have everlasting life
(John 3:16).

. . . God sent his only begotten Son into the
world, that we might live through him. Herein
is love, not that we loved God, but that he loved
us, and sent his Son to be the propitiation for
our sins (1 John 4:9–10).

Behold, what manner of love the Father hath
bestowed upon us, that we should be called the
sons of God . . . (1 John 3:1).

Nor height, nor depth, nor any other creature,
shall be able to separate us from the love of

God, which is in Christ Jesus our Lord (Romans 8:39).

Can our minds comprehend the mystery and marvel of it all? How shall we explain such divine prodigality? "And all they that heard it wondered at those things which were told them by the shepherds" (Luke 2:18). And so do we. We can say only that God loves us as He does because He is God, and we can shout with joy that He cared enough to send His greatest blessing!

There is so much about us that speaks in a different, and an indifferent, tongue. The accent of the universe is one of dispassionate impartiality. Not so with God. His accent is one of passionate partiality—even for us.

God loves us because He hopes thereby to claim us for Himself, to save us from the stupidity of treadmill living and from the foolishness and folly of our sinfulness, and to raise us from our split-level living to the height and nobility of heroic and victorious spiritual achievement.

And what can we do about it?

> Love so amazing, so divine,
> Demands my soul, my life, my all.

We may respond with all we have got to give. When God woos us with such loving compassion, can we turn from Him?

Christmas is also a love story because of Joseph, who rose above his questionings and doubts and gave himself heart and soul to Mary whom God had chosen as a worthy vessel by which His love might be made manifest. We could have understood if Joseph had turned from Mary, but he did not. His faith transcended his misgivings. He enfolded her helplessness in his strong arms after God's messenger had said, "Joseph, thou son of David, fear not to take unto thee Mary thy wife: for that which is conceived in her is of the Holy Ghost" (Matthew 1:20).

Joseph ministered to Mary's needs as they made their tiresome pilgrimage from Nazareth to Bethlehem for the enrollment ordered by Caesar Augustus. He sought reposeful quarters for her, and when her hour had come, he was at her side. For her safety he led her and the Child to a distant land beyond the reach of Herod's wrath. Later he guided them back to his home in the hills where he devotedly provided a home which, though perhaps unostentatious, knew such comfort and protection as only self-effacing love offers. The love of God is mirrored in the heart of the rugged carpenter of Nazareth.

Christmas, furthermore, is a love story because Mary cradled the Child in the arms of a tender and dedicated love. The life of Mary is an exquisite tapestry woven with those golden threads which we find in all loving and sacrificial motherhood.

The Lord of highest heaven, whose creativity is proclaimed by the spacious firmament, whose power is flaunted in orbiting spheres, and whose sovereignty no man can gainsay, unveiled His love in a Babe reared with loving care and concern within a home. God thereby made holy the hearth, and He hallowed the family altar. Since that distant day the life within the family circle has been sacramental.

Christmas is a family day. "Home for Christmas" are the words on the lips of earth's prodigal children. This is a day for joyous family reunions, a day when, perhaps more so than on any other day, young and old rejoice in each other's good company. This is also the day when we remember especially the vanished voices and the empty chairs at the Christmas table.

When Christmas came to Bethlehem, love came too. And Jesus, who was cradled in the arms of Mary's love, has ever since blessed all families and tightened the bonds of Christian love. And He has stretched our hearts to enclose all men within the circumference of our love, for He teaches us that God has "got the whole world in His hands."

The elemental lesson in the school of Christ is that we love Him because He first loved us, and that we love others, both the lovable and the unlovable, in His name.

Don't let this Christmas pass by without realizing the challenges and compulsions on the frontiers of Christian love. The old and familiar words of Kate Douglas Wiggin are worthy of remembrance:

> My heart is open wide to-night
> To stranger, kith or kin.
> I would not bar a single door
> Where Love might enter in.

29

The Forgotten Man at Bethlehem

A worried mother phoned the church office on the afternoon before the annual Christmas party of the Sunday school to say that her small son, who was to play the role of Joseph in the Christmas play, had a cold and had gone to bed on doctor's orders. "It is too late now to get another Joseph," the teacher replied. "We'll just have to write him out of the script." And they did, and very few of those who watched the play that night realized that the cast was incomplete.

Joseph of Nazareth is the most neglected person in the Christmas story. Who would think of Christmas without singing angels, bright-eyed shepherds, sedate and regal Wise Men, a pompous and blustering Herod, or even a frantic and nervous innkeeper? We couldn't have Christmas without them! But Joseph—well, we often write him out of the script.

Maybe our ignoring of Joseph is something most fathers can understand. "Good old dad" nods resignedly when his children clamor for new clothes. He tags along when mother goes to school to check on Johnny's grades. He stays in the car while the family does the shopping. He waits in the next room as the children share their little confidences with mother.

He twiddles his thumbs helplessly in the hospital lobby when his children are being delivered, and he feels somehow neglected and out of place at his daughter's wedding party.

Perhaps we excuse our forgetfulness of Joseph in sermons, song, art and verse by saying that, after all, Joseph was a pretty common man who added very little to the excitement and spectacle of the gospel story.

Joseph's hands were calloused by his toil in a little carpentry shop in Nazareth. He never wrote his memoirs. He didn't utter imperishable words—nowhere in the Bible is a single word of his quoted. He looked with awe upon the wisdom of those who had mastered ancient lore, and he profoundly respected those who spoke with an erudite authority which was incomprehensible to one having his limited schooling.

The word "ordinary" describes Joseph. And who ever gets excited over such persons? Who—except, perhaps, God? God, who is no respecter of persons, looks benevolently upon all men. To him no man is mean or common. The word "ordinary" is not to be found in the vocabulary of Deity.

If the landscape of Joseph's world was horizontally cramped and confining, his skyscape knew no limitations, for his soul was ever sensitive to and also responsive to things spiritual. God was no stranger to his heart. He knew the diction and syntax of eternity. When God spoke, Joseph understood and obeyed. His mind was infiltrated with a glory of a higher sphere.

There is a man like Joseph in every church. He is

faithful, dependable, helpful and considerate. He makes no splash and draws no attention to himself, but he turns off the lights when the others have left, he locks the door, and he takes home a heart heavy with the burdens of others. And "of such is the kingdom of heaven" (Matthew 19:14)!

Men like Joseph are the salt of the earth and the yeast in the dough. They are the key logs in the jam of human relationships. H. G. Wells may well have had such men in mind when he wrote, "There dwell eternal gallantries and eternal generosities within the heart of man." And God knows how to detect strength in meekness and to employ obscure saints in His Kingdom.

"What kind of a preacher do you have?" a man asked an acquaintance. "He is a lighter of lamps in a dark world," was the reply. This is the kind of person Joseph was, and the lamps he lighted still shine brightly. We would do well to remember this forgotten man at Bethlehem. He is a person we should know more about.

If an epitaph were to be chosen to identify the final resting place of Joseph, these words would be particularly appropriate:

A JUST MAN

And these are the very words Matthew uses to describe Joseph.

Little information about him may be gleaned from the Gospels. The occasional references to him are like pieces of a crossword puzzle which must be patiently arranged if a portrait is to emerge. When, however, this has been accomplished, we have before us an individual who is worthy of our praise and veneration.

In the gospels we read that Joseph, after he had become engaged to Mary, discovered that she was anticipating the birth of her first child. Before he was told the truth regarding her situation, he considered the possibility of severing his betrothal in such a way that she might not be unduly disgraced or shamed. Then God revealed to this godly man His eternal purpose which would be made evident in the birth of Mary's son.

Joseph then gladly became her husband, attended her at the hour of Christ's birth, arranged for the safety of mother and Child during their flight into Egypt, and later provided both a home and companionship for the Lad.

By heritage, Joseph was in the royal lineage of King David. By vocation, he was a carpenter. Because no direct reference is made concerning him after Jesus' twelfth year, we may presume that he died when Jesus was still young.

Matthew speaks of Joseph as being "a just man." These words may be translated as "a righteous man." "Righteousness" in those days was a stronger word than it is in our common usage. "Righteousness" meant uprightness before God. Joseph lived to the best of his ability in a right relationship with God.

Something of the righteousness of Joseph may be suggested to us by Jesus' own teaching regarding man's duty and responsibility to God. Through the ministries of Jesus the words and disciplines of

Joseph have permeated the centuries. Who can fully measure the good which issues from the life of a just and righteous person?

When Christmas came to Bethlehem, Joseph of Nazareth found a purpose for his life within the greater purposes of God. And so may we. When we link our little lives to God, we become uncommonly essential in the economy of eternity.

30

Christmas at Their Doorstep

Joseph and Mary journeyed eighty-five miles along dusty roads from Nazareth to David's City for the Roman enrollment. The Wise Men, following caravan routes which were ancient even in Solomon's day, traveled untold distances from their far-flung oriental kingdoms. But the shepherds of Bethlehem bowed reverently at the manger of the Christ Child who was born within the range of their voices. Christmas at their doorstep! How very fortunate they were! And on a night when they least expected it, they were singled out for an everlasting glory in music and art and poetry.

These hearty men of Bethlehem were tending their flocks when an angel of the Lord appeared unto them. Nothing like that had ever happened to them before. In fact, nothing much ever happened to disturb the monotony of their lives. Occasionally, of course, a rustle among the flocks made it evident that an intruder, perhaps a wolf, lurked nearby. But when the danger passed, the shepherds piped softly a tune on their reed instruments and the sheep became calm once more. The shepherds then sang a folk song their fathers had taught them, or passed the never-ending hours of their nightly vigil swapping grandfather stories and munching on olives, bread and dried figs.

But this night was unlike all of the others. The sky became radiant with a light not of this world. Read again the words of the time-cherished story as found in Luke 2:9–14:

> And, lo, the angel of the Lord came upon them, and the glory of the Lord shone round about them: and they were sore afraid. And the angel said unto them, Fear not: for, behold, I bring you good tidings of great joy, which shall be to all people. For unto you is born this day in the city of David a Saviour, which is Christ the Lord . . . . And suddenly there was with the angel a multitude of the heavenly host praising God, and saying, Glory to God in the highest, and on earth peace, good will toward men.

Glory be! Such a great honor for so small a town. Such a tremendous message for the ears of common men. But why not? Were not these very likely the same fields where Israel's hero, David, had once tended flocks and sung of green pastures, still waters, and divine guidance through the valley? God had returned to His favorite people, the shepherd folk from whom Abraham, Moses, Amos, and a host of other spiritual giants had come. To these common men who had for generations bred spotless and unblemished lambs for temple sacrifices came the proclamation of the Good Shepherd and of the Lamb of God which taketh away the sins of the world.

Naturally the shepherds were fearful when the shadows were pierced with light and a celestial choir, the first Christmas carollers, made the heavens quiver with a message of God's love. What a magnificent memory would be forever enshrined within the memories of those shepherd lads!

But their fears did not long persist. At the angel's bidding, they went "with haste" to see for themselves "this thing which is come to pass, which the Lord hath made known . . ." (Luke 2:15–16). The words "with haste" are meaningful. The shepherds did not hesitate, nor quibble over questions and doubts, nor prolong their decision until a more convenient season. One of the splendid things about those shepherds, who were wise in a lore not gleaned from books, was that, when God spoke, they did not dillydally but rather responded with a wholesome spontaneity which puts to shame our misgivings, qualifications, reservations and equivocations when God calls to us.

"Let us now go . . . and see." Well, they may well have reasoned, we have nothing to lose and possibly everything to gain. Were the good tidings too good to be true? Nay, too good not to be true. And they found Him whom they sought!

There are arresting and challenging aspects in the experience of those shepherds. First, the glorious news came when they were engaged in their common chores. A shepherd's work was not exciting.

> In summer's heat, and winter's cold,
> He fed his flock, and penn'd the fold.

Probably the Judean shepherds would long before have escaped from their tedious labors if they could have, but they couldn't. And often we can't either, however beckoning may be all that lies beyond the horizon. We have our work to do and responsibilities we cannot shrug off. Contented or not with our lot in life, we have no alternative other than to do the task at hand, which, if we are not diligent, will never get done.

How often God comes when we least expect Him and when we plod on with never a hope to see a heavenly light. Gideon was threshing wheat when God commissioned him, Saul was looking for domestic animals which had strayed from home, Elisha was plowing with twelve yoke of oxen, and Amos was picking the fruit of sycamore trees. None anticipated a heavenly visitation in such unlikely situations.

Do we scorn our lowly stations and our humdrum labors? The arms of heavenly love enfolded the shepherds as they, perhaps in quiet desperation, pursued their daily work with all the wit and courage they could muster. A glory surrounds our most common tasks when we are workmen who are not ashamed of what we do or of the quality of our achievements. Dr. Albert Schweitzer has written, "Plenty of people write to me in hope of getting some spectacular work to do and at the same time they fail to see the worthwhileness of the immediate duty given them." Because of their faithfulness, the shepherds were redeemed from smallness by God who calls no good work mediocre.

Second, to the shepherds of Bethlehem was spoken

the most glorious word in the vocabulary of Christmas. That word is *joy*. ". . . behold, I bring you good tidings of great joy . . ." (Luke 2:10).

The New Testament is the most hopeful Book in the world. It reverberates with an exultant, triumphant and victorious joy that surges, permeates and penetrates. The story of creation exhibits " a lip-smacking, exuberant delight in the ingenious beauty and variety of the created world"; the New Testament throbs with such joyous words as these: "Now the God of hope fill you with all joy and peace in believing . . ." (Romans 15:13).

If the Bible is the most joyful of all books, Christians should surely be the most joyous of people. Sometimes we are not. Yet the Christian who is a sourpuss has read well neither the signs in the heavens nor the Word of the Lord. Do we too easily resign ourselves to life's buffetings? Resignation is a stoic, not a Christian virtue. Are there frustrations which prayer and fasting do not seem to remove? Are there intolerable situations or, even worse, intolerable persons with whom we are inescapably associated? These a Christian accepts, if he must, and his acceptance is uplifted by a song. For however hard may be the Christian way, both in the traveling and in the attaining of the goal, it is a way of joy. "The Christian is the laughing cavalier of Christ."

This joy is derivative. It is a gift from God in Christ. Our Lord said, "These things have I spoken unto you, that my joy might remain in you, and that your joy might be full" (John 15:11). Genuine joy is a divine legacy. We do not shop for it at the bargain counter in an end-of-the-year clearance sale. Our joy is a confidence born of our trust in God. We are, as Christians, held responsible to "maintain the spiritual glow" (Romans 12:11, MOFFATT).

This joy is also reciprocal. Real joy is a contagious thing, something we receive that we may then share it. ". . . such as I have give I thee" (Acts 3:6).

The word of joy came to the shepherds in the line of duty. And so it comes to us.

Third, after the shepherds had stood in hushed silence before God's revelation in a manger, they did something about it. They became men with a mission. Too often we adore the Baby, and that is all. Nothing happens to us, for nothing happens in us. The wonder of it impels us to—nothing. Not so the shepherds: "And when they had seen it, they made known abroad the saying which was told them concerning this child" (Luke 2:17). Their joy motivated action. Not only were they the first to be told; they were also the first to tell. In a lively sense, their witness that night made them the first Christian missionaries. These troubadours of God had found something they could not fold carefully in a napkin and bury in a hole.

We come with anticipation to the crib. We must not stop on dead center. Let us go forth to seek and to save. Let us not settle for half a loaf. Sometimes we are pretty miserly about our faith. Real joy always shows, and something ought to rub off in our enthusiasm, in our commitment, in our testimony, and in our desire to share and serve.

An attractive travel brochure, which has come in the mail, invites us to spend Christmas Eve in Bethlehem.

That would be wonderful. But if we lack time or money, are we deprived of the shepherds' joy? Not at all, for, if we will, Christmas will come to us.

> Into my heart, into my heart,
> Come into my heart, Lord Jesus;
> Come in today, come in to stay,
> Come into my heart, Lord Jesus.

And if we welcome Him, He will enter, for He stands at our doorstep.

31

A Long Day's Journey Into Light

Does anyone really question whether or not the birth of Jesus is the inexpressibly important event in the history of man? His coming is the great watershed in the chronicle of humanity. We cannot, if we wish, be indifferent to Him. Even our calendars—split between the years before and following His birth—mock our apathy.

But why is His birth of such great consequence? After twenty centuries, why do more than 900 million human beings in every coast and clime honor and reverence Him? By way of suggesting an answer, let us center our thoughts on a poem by one of our distinguished contemporary poets, "Journey of the Magi," by T. S. Eliot. As in all excellent poetry, this poem with verve and clarity probes deeply and lays bare eternal truth.

One of the Magi, now old in years and rich in experience, recalls that day long ago when with the others he crossed sand-blown wastelands in pursuit of a beckoning, challenging star:

> A cold coming we had of it,
> Just the worst time of year

> For a journey, and such a long journey:
> The ways deep and the weather sharp,
> The very dead of winter.

At times during that pilgrimage he remembered the pleasures of the home he had left:

> The summer palaces on slopes, the terraces,
> And the silken girls bringing sherbet.

And, of course, there were those strangers along the way who taunted him by jeering that his journey was all folly.

> All this was a long time ago,

muses the Magi, who asks,

> Were we led all that way for
> Birth or Death?

He had seen births and deaths before, but

> . . . this Birth was
> Hard and bitter agony for us, like Death, our death.

When he returned once again to his own kingdom, he was a changed man. The old routines and treasured beliefs no longer satisfied him. At Bethlehem all that had died. Something new had been born in him.

The short poem concludes as the old man declares:

I should be glad of another death.

By this he means that he would gladly die again if he might discover anew that kind of spiritual birth.

Such is the substance of Mr. Eliot's poem, but a poem is always more than words and images. It is an impression on the mind, a seed that matures in the imagination, a leaf borne gently on the winds of experience. And this poem suggests far more than it states. It unfolds the true meaning of Christmas. A man of questing faith must give up some things if his life is to be enlarged with new truth, or indeed by Him who is the Truth.

If we come to Christmas burdened with fears and doubts, anxieties and shriveled minds, we shall never know Him who is the Way, the Truth and the Life. These things must go. They must die, if something new—the life and light of God revealed in the Son of His love—is to be born within our hearts.

Jesus said, "Marvel not that I said unto thee, Ye must be born again" (John 3:7). When His life and spirit are born within us, we shall never regret the death of all that we previously may have coveted. Jesus teaches us in words charged with a never-ending pertinence: "Verily, verily, I say unto you, He that heareth my word, and believeth on him that sent me, hath everlasting life, and shall not come into condemnation; but is passed from death unto life" (John 5:24).

To revise slightly, yet significantly, the title of

Eugene O'Neill's agonizing autobiographical drama, the Magi set out upon a long day's journey into light. And that light may be ours too, if we focus the vision of our hearts upon Bethlehem and Him who is the Light of the World. ". . . if any man be in Christ, he is a new creature: old things are passed away; behold, all things are become new" (2 Corinthians 5:17).

32

The Man Who Missed Christmas

Herod is no stranger to the twentieth century. Cut from the same cloth of tyranny as the dictators of our generation, Herod climbed the stepping-stones of bribery and butchery to a powerful position that corrupted him and drained from his heart the last lingering vestige of love and compassion. Ultimately, he bequeathed to his people a legacy of bitterness and bloodshed.

Herod became governor of Galilee at the age of twenty-five. He so ingratiated himself with Anthony and Octavius that they appointed him as king. The Roman senate subsequently conferred upon him the title "King of the Jews."

Historical records have distinguished him with the innocuous words of "Herod the Great," for although he was a puppet-ruler and beholden to Roman caprice and whim, he undertook stupendous building enterprises including the building of cities, amphitheaters and pagan temples. His most ambitious plans centered in the building upon Zerubbabel's foundations of the great temple in Jerusalem, a magnificent structure wherein Jesus worshiped. Like many another crafty politician, Herod curried popular favor by offering something to everyone—Roman, Jew and Gentile.

When the Wise Men asked concerning the place where Christ should be born, Herod could not answer. But waving his hand toward Bethlehem, he urged them on their way, saying, "Go and search diligently for the young child; and when ye have found him, bring me word again, that I may come and worship him also" (Matthew 2:8).

Of course, Herod had no intention of worshiping the Child. Although he lived in a house of mirrors and feasted on self-adulation, the slightest hint that there might be within his realm a potential rival to his iron-fisted rule brought grave misgivings to his suspicion-tortured mind. Did he dispatch secret agents to dog the steps of the Wise Men? That would have been in character!

Herod shrouded himself in a fog of piety and pretense by saying, ". . . bring me word again, that I may come and worship him also." But even as the silhouettes of the Wise Men faded on the road to Bethlehem, Herod set in motion an ingenious scheme which he believed would forever remove whatever threat to his reign the birth of the Child might portend. He gave orders which brought an unbearable heartache into a multitude of homes: "Then Herod, when he saw that he was mocked of the wise men, was exceeding wroth, and sent forth, and slew all the children that were in Bethlehem, and in all the coasts thereof, from two years old and under, according to the time which he had diligently enquired of the wise men" (Matthew 2:16). The Slaughter of the Innocents was a typical Herodian gesture. Had not fear and sus-

picion long before corroded his mind? When, so he
thought, the shadow of intrigue had fallen upon his
wife Mariamne, he ordered her execution and that of
her two sons by him. The carpet upon which he trod
was blood-red with innocent blood.

Men of Herod's stature can brook no opposition.
Tyranny always behaves in a similar fashion. In our
day we have seen the machinations of dictators who
have destroyed all dissenters and exiled or murdered
all opponents. No other way is open to them, for they
have secured their power by force and they know that
always there is the possibility that another force may
topple them. ". . . all they that take the sword shall
perish with the sword" (Matthew 26:52). Nothing is as
unstable as a government built only upon might and
power.

Down the centuries there have been those who
have been afraid of Christ's coming, and those who
have known their fondest hopes to be fulfilled in Him.
The story of Christianity is a chronicle of those who
have rejected and those who have accepted the Son of
God.

The birth of the Christ Child did threaten the rule of
Herod, but not in the way Herod imagined. Herod
believed that the Child would grow into an ardent and
persuasive military leader who would link forces with
the multitudes of persons who long had suffered
under the yoke of despotism. Retributive justice is
deeply woven into the fabric of history, and this
Herod knew. A few years, and the Child might con-
ceivably become the champion of an irresistible force

so potent and powerful that the mercenaries of Herod would be helpless to resist them.

But the Kingdom which Christ's birth promised was not one which the sick mind of Herod could comprehend. To be sure, Christ would rally to His standard millions of discontented peoples, but not for a military struggle nor for armed conflict. Christ's mission was to become a spiritual engagement against the entrenched battalions of wickedness. He would lead but not compel. His would be an army of volunteers whose only weapon would be the power of love.

We who worship the Child have every reason to rejoice with exceeding great joy, for we are citizens of a Kingdom of compassion and salvation. And we even now perceive the foregleams of that day when the kingdoms of the Herods of this world shall become the kingdoms of our Lord, and of His Christ, and He shall reign forever and ever.

Of those persons cast in the drama of the nativity only King Herod did not go to Bethlehem. Herod remained behind and sought diversions to calm his troubled mind. *He was the man who missed Christmas.*

Ironically, he missed what might well have been his golden hour, the privilege of culminating his thirty-three-year reign by laying his crown at the Child's feet. Shortly after the radiant star above Bethlehem faded from sight, death, the inexorable fate of all mortals, brought to an end Herod's life. Knowing that his subjects would rejoice to hear the news of his death, Herod provided that many influential Jews should be executed on the day he died, thereby assuring a general lamentation throughout Judea. But those charged with so fearsome a responsibility relented, and when Herod did at last die there was instead a widespread jubilation as is known only among those freed from a long and dismal captivity.

The pomp and power of Herod's reign is now a diminished thing, and he is remembered today only because of his minor role as villain in the drama of human salvation.

Shelley described an inscription on a weather- and sand-worn monument in the desert:

> "My name is Ozymandias, king of kings:
> Look on my works, ye Mighty, and despair!"

Then the poet adds a telling comment:

> Nothing beside remains. Round the decay
> Of that colossal wreck, boundless and bare
> The lone and level sands stretch far away.

Of the Herods who noisily strut across the pages of history, one thing only is certain—and that is their impermanence. "Towering o'er the wrecks of time" is that dominion not made with hands whose King reigns by love and rules in mercy. ". . . and he shall reign for ever and ever" (Revelation 11:15).

33

Living Expectantly

Eight days after the glory had faded from the skies above Bethlehem and the shepherds had returned to their flocks, Joseph and Mary journeyed to Jerusalem in order that Mary's firstborn might be dedicated to the Lord according to the requirement of the ancient law.

Can we, with kindled imaginations, visualize their pilgrimage to the magnificent temple? What thoughts surged within their hearts as these country folk looked upon the great white marble edifice whose gold-burnished walls reflected the glory of the sun? Were their spirits on tiptoe with wonder as they secured the sacrifice stipulated for the poor, a pair of turtledoves, and then prepared their offering?

The quiet of this holy hour was interrupted by the approach of a Spirit-led stranger, a righteous and devout man named Simeon, whose kindly face was traced with wrinkles and whose white hair tumbled to his shoulders. He took the Child gently in his hands and blessed God.

This was for Simeon a moment of supreme joy, for he had longed for the day, now fulfilled, when his eyes should feast upon Him who would bring to pass the messianic hope that had budded and flowered through four thousand years in the hearts of pious men. The divine Spirit had assured Simeon that he would not join his fathers in death until after this beatific hour had come.

All of his hopes having centered in the Child's coming, Simeon now turned to that peace beyond the Jordan which crowns the life of the faithful. His swan song, known in Christian liturgy as the *Nunc Dimittis,* which in Latin means "now lettest thou depart," has been a blessing and a benediction to Christians for nearly twenty centuries:

> Lord, now lettest thou thy servant depart in peace, according to thy word: For mine eyes have seen thy salvation, Which thou hast prepared before the face of all people; A light to lighten the Gentiles, and the glory of thy people Israel (Luke 2:29–32).

At that moment the trio from Bethlehem were joined by Anna, a holy woman of eighty-four years, who, like Simeon, had kept aflame in her heart the hope of the redemption of Jerusalem. She gazed in rapturous wonder upon the Child and then proclaimed Him to be the long-awaited Messiah and the Fulfiller of the ancient promises.

A few bold and glowing strokes from the evangelist's pen record all we may know of Simeon and Anna. Yet infinitely more is suggested than the words reveal. Throughout Israel's long and turbulent history faithful persons, at times a mere handful, clung to the assurance of deliverance. They lived, not by their doubts and fears, but by their soaring anticipations and heaven-borne aspirations.

Some men are chained within the shadows of yesterday's calamities, and some are imprisoned by old failures. Others live for tomorrow. This aging couple, old in the accumulation of years, were young in heart and hope. Tennyson in "Ulysses" wrote, "Old age hath yet his honor and his toil." Hope is not the coveted treasure only of the young. Within the dim eyes of these temple habitués was the vision of a coming glory.

They had read perceptively and receptively the pages of the ancient Scriptures, and they found there an ever-growing expectation of the messianic hope which is a golden thread binding the hearts of Abraham, Isaac, David, the Psalmists, Isaiah, Micah, and many others. God in His own good season would redeem His people through "the anointed one." So it was revealed to Simeon and Anna when the lens of ancient prophecy zeroed in on Bethlehem and the birth of Christ, whose name is the Greek equivalent for the Hebrew word *messiah*.

> The hopes and fears of all the years
> Are met in thee tonight.

Among the personalities in the nativity story, only Simeon and Anna understood precisely the role in which the Child had been cast. Did the Wise Men comprehend the historical and eternal meaning of Christ's coming? Probably not. Did the shepherds share this insight? Probably not. Could Herod have fathomed the divine purpose of the newborn king? Probably not. But Simeon and Anna knew, and their patient watchfulness and waiting—the vigil of their anxious hearts—were rewarded. Although they surely did not live to witness the completion of Christ's divinely ordained ministry on Calvary, they died in peace, having seen the King who reigns in love and rules by serving, the Deliverer who liberates, and the Saviour who rescues.

Simeon and Anna personify all people, young and old and of every generation, our own not excluded, whose lives are patterned by great expectations for the redemption, not only of Jerusalem, but of mankind.

The word "redemption" is not in the vocabulary of many present-day Christians, although the word is hallowed by its use in the Bible and in traditional Christian theology. Redemption means to be redeemed, as we might redeem an obligation, or to set free. Man is bound by sin and death. He is helpless to free himself. Only God can release man from his bondage. Simeon and Anna, like their spiritual ancestors, anticipated the day when by God's grace man would be emancipated from his slavery to sin.

The redemption realized through Christ did not come without the payment of a heavy price. Only by being crushed upon the cross could Jesus fulfill the promise of old. The cross can be understood only in terms of the love of God for His sinful children. In His self-giving on the cross Jesus bore upon Himself the sins of men and reconciled humanity to a heavenly

Father from whom they had been estranged by their disobedience.

The angel of the Lord appeared unto Joseph, saying that Mary's child should be called Jesus, "for he shall save his people from their sins" (Matthew 1:21). Paul affirmed that "Christ Jesus came into the world to save sinners . . ." (1 Timothy 1:15). This salvation came through the teachings of Jesus, through the example of His life, and supremely through His death. "For when we were yet without strength, in due time Christ died for the ungodly" (Romans 5:6).

Simeon and Anna enter the gospel story unobtrusively and quietly, and in a moment pass into the silences of time, but they have left for us worthy examples of the power and comfort of great expectations.

34

Don't Blame the Innkeeper!

After the birth of Jesus, His mother laid Him on the soft straw in a shed or cave where animals were customarily sheltered. Such a circumstance seems hardly appropriate for the most revered and beloved Man ever to share the habiliment of our mortality. But the evangelist's explanation is simple and to the point: ". . . there was no room for them in the inn" (Luke 2:7).

We do not know how many native-born Bethlehemites returned to register for the census, but the number surely was considerable and the housing facilities of the community were insufficient even for an open-hearted people who had traditionally cultivated hospitality as an art and responsibility.

Joseph of Nazareth had no doubt anticipated lodgings in the only travelers' lodge of which Bethlehem could boast. Perhaps he had stayed there before. But when he rapped at the doorpost, he was told that he had arrived too late for accommodations.

Luke does not say that the innkeeper spoke with Joseph. In fact, he does not even mention an innkeeper, although we presume that he came forward to suggest that the travelers from Nazareth were welcome to whatever comfort and protection the stable might afford. And that wasn't too bad, for undoubtedly both Joseph and Mary, according to the custom of their day, would have been used to the practice of bringing domestic beasts into their home each evening.

Subsequent literary invention, however, has scorned the anonymous innkeeper for his callousness in turning the Nazarenes from his door. He has been castigated in poetry and prose and cast in a role similar to that of the villain of a second-rate Western saga. Ralph W. Seager generously suggests in his poem "The Wisest of the Wise" that there is another side of the coin:

> I'll stand beside the keeper of the inn,
> Challenging those who charge him with the sin
> That let the Child be born within his stable.
> I say he did the best that he was able,
> Under the circumstance. Where else would there
> Be privacy and summer-scented air?
> The beasts, benign in their nobility,
> Stood watch; and this, at least it seems to me,
> Gave courtesy unto the act of birth.
> The hostel must have reeled with raucous mirth,
> Jangling the laden night with feast and dance
> As Roman taxes found the dice of chance.
> Only a wise man would have seen the manger
> As a cradle beyond the pry of stranger.
> When pompous fingers shame his guiltless deed,
> I'm on his side, disciple of the need
> To say he was the wisest one of all,
> Providing the sanctuary of the stall.

Does not this poet more correctly interpret the innkeeper than do those who have portrayed him as the
Mr. Scrooge of Bethlehem?

This innkeeper, whose work had schooled him to be
friendly and hospitable, had no way of knowing that
Mary bore a precious treasure. No divine messenger
conveyed to him the marvelous words which Joseph
and Mary pondered in their hearts, no angelic choir
sang to him, and no star guided his steps. And even if
he had seen or heard such wonders, there remains the
unalterable fact that there was no room for them in the
inn.

The Scriptures do not offer the slightest hint that
Joseph felt unkindly toward the innkeeper. Learning
of the circumstances, Joseph was humbly grateful for
the friendly hand that led him to the stable. Our scorn,
if we must be scornful, should be directed toward
those who, in later years and even nowadays, turn the
Lord of life from their homes and hearts.

One of the tragic minor chords in the New Testament is found in John 1:10–11: "He was in the world,
and the world was made by him, and the world knew
him not. He came unto his own, and his own received
him not." Someone wrote concerning a great American naturalist and botanist: "He loved gardens, but he
did not know the Gardener."

Many who sing the beautiful carols of this season
have no real knowledge of Christ. Or their acquaintance with Him is casual, or their attitude is diffident.
They attend His birthday parties without much caring
about Him. Their ears are unresponsive to the solicita-
tions and entreaties of the Christmas Host.

Even more pathetic are those persons who, once having loved Christ, have permitted their ardor to cool. They do nothing to nurture and sustain their friendship with the one true and eternal Friend. Their Christmas celebration is little more than a lingering legacy of a once-living companionship.

When we make room in our lives for Christ, He in turn fills our souls with the greatest of all blessings—a genuine relationship and kinship with God. "But as many as received him, to them gave he power to become the sons of God, even to them that believe on his name" (John 1:12).

35

Where Shall We Find Him?

When the Wise Men had come to Jerusalem, they asked, "Where is he that is born King of the Jews? for we have seen his star in the east, and are come to worship him" (Matthew 2:2). Whom did they ask? We do not know. The Scriptures are silent at this point.

We do know that their travel to Bethlehem had been on no magic carpet and that no automobile association sped them on their way again. *But they did find Bethlehem.* Someone in that teeming capital city of Judea gave them the answer they sought.

Perhaps some youngster, whose eyes had been lured by an unknown celestial light, pointed them toward Bethlehem, five short miles as the crow flies to the south. Or perhaps a man in the flower of youth and, like them, a knight of spiritual adventuring and derring-do, agreed to accompany them. Or perhaps a man of advancing years, his sight too dim now to read the heavens, recalled having read in the ancient scroll of Micah a messianic promise to which his heart still clung: "But thou, Bethlehem Ephratah, though thou be little among the thousands of Judah, yet out of thee shall he come forth unto me that is to be ruler in Israel; whose goings forth have been from old, from everlasting" (Micah 5:2).

Someone, no doubt an obscure passerby, knew the answer, and so the Wise Men continued on the last lap of their pilgrimage.

In the days which followed, men were ever seeking Jesus. Certain of the Jews asked of the brethren of Jesus, "Where is he?" (John 7:11). The neighbors of the man born blind, whose sight Jesus restored, questioned him concerning the One who had anointed his eyes with healing, and then they asked concerning the Healer, "Where is he?" (John 9:12). To Philip the Greeks said with insistence, "Sir, we would see Jesus" (John 12:21). After having found Jesus in a solitary sanctuary of prayer, the disciples exclaimed to their Master, "All men seek for thee" (Mark 1:37). At the door of the tomb on the first Easter morning, an angel said to the faithful women, "Fear not ye: for I know that ye seek Jesus . . ." (Matthew 28:5).

Even as He was sought after during His ministry in the flesh, so do men today seek to find Him. Where shall we find Him? At this season we are especially reminded that within the whole span of life there is no more important question.

Some wise men of our generation have wondered aloud whether He really can be found. Edwin Arlington Robinson in his poem "Credo" laments:

> I cannot find my way: there is no star
> In all the shrouded heavens anywhere.

And Archibald MacLeish in *J.B.*, his twentieth-century redaction of the story of Job, bemoans a spiritual climate that hangs heavily over our day:

The candles in churches are out.
The lights have gone out in the sky.

Is there any hope at all that we may find Christ? Will our searching bring us to Him?

Herod missed seeing the Child, but the Wise Men and the shepherds were not disappointed in their quests. There is a chance that we shall miss Him altogether. It could be that we shall become so encumbered in our multitude of Yuletime activities that we shall be exhausted before we get to Bethlehem. Or maybe we shall let others search for Him for us, and await whatever word they may bring back. This is what Herod did, and the Wise Men bypassed him on their journey home. Or our hard hearts may be so flooded with doubt and skepticism that we shall hesitate to believe with our minds what our spirits affirm.

Of this we may be certain: if we fail to find Christ in this season of joyous faith, we shall have little more than a synthetic Christmas. What a tragedy to exchange cards, gifts and greetings, but not to know the radiance of stardust!

To be sure, we shall not now find Him in a crib. He was a Child for only a handful of fleeting years. Nor shall we find Him walking along some hallowed pathway in Palestine. He long since passed from the familiar shores of Galilee. Nor shall we gaze at Him upon a cross or within the dark recesses of a tomb. The cross claimed Him for a narrow day, and the tomb could not bind Him.

Of none other whose name is inscribed upon the

annals of history is it said that, having been raised from the dead, He dieth no more. ". . . death hath no more dominion over him" (Romans 6:9). The testimony and witness of Christianity is that Christ, though slain by spiritual astigmatism and malignant hate, defied death and rose to everlasting life.

This is a mystery which befuddles our power of explanation and interpretation. Yet, upon this truth, vindicated in the experience of many generations of believers, is established the gospel and the glory of our faith.

And of none other who has shared the garments of mortal flesh is it affirmed that He is a living Personality who may be our constant Companion and ever-living Friend.

By faith Christ lives within our hearts. His Spirit is closer to us than our own hands and feet. He has assured us, "I am with you alway . . ." (Matthew 28:20). Paul wrote, ". . . I live; yet not I, but Christ liveth in me . . ." (Galatians 2:20). ". . . we dwell in him, and he in us . . ." (1 John 4:13). Katharine Lee Bates telescopes a vast truth into four brief lines:

> Not the Christ in the manger,
> Not the Christ on the Cross;
> But the Christ in the soul,
> When all but love is lost.

This is the supreme and redeeming word which the Christmas message should bring home to each of us: not that we must still seek a Babe in a crib He outgrew, nor a Teacher who has now moved from the classrooms of Galilee, nor an exhausted Saviour stretched upon a cross, nor a Leader wrapped in the soft linens of death, but rather ". . . Christ in you, the hope of glory" (Colossians 1:27).